GLOBAL EDGE

Joel Kurtzman
Glenn Yago

GLOBAL EDGE

Using the Opacity Index to Manage the
Risks of Cross-Border Business

Harvard Business School Press

Boston, Massachusetts

HD
62.4
.IC873
2007

MIC Printed in the United States of America

11 10 09 08 07   5 4 3 2 1

Library of Congress Cataloging-in-Publication Data
Kurtzman, Joel.
  Global edge : using the opacity index to manage the risks of cross-border business / Joel Kurtzman, Glenn Yago.
      p. cm.
  Includes bibliographical references.
  ISBN-13: 978-1-4221-0346-3 (hardcover : alk. paper)
  ISBN-10: 1-4221-0346-3
  1. International business enterprises--Management. 2. Risk management. 3. Globalization--Economic aspects. 4. International trade. I. Yago, Glenn. II. Title.
  HD62.4.K873 2007
  658.15'5—dc22

                           2007014158

The paper used in this publication meets the requirements of the American National Standard for Permanence of Paper for Publications and Documents in Libraries and Archives Z39.48-1992.

To our wives, Karen Warner and Stephanie Yago, and to our children. May they live in a world of less risk and more transparency.

And what will clearer vision do for people, in the main?
Will our thoughts extrapolate like links within a chain?
It would be nice, when looking at a galaxy or star,
To see the cosmos' vastness, and how minuscule we are.

—David Arns, "I Can See Clearly Now," *Quantum*

Contents

Preface and Acknowledgments

In October 1999, James Schiro, the visionary former chief executive of PricewaterhouseCoopers and current CEO of Zurich Financial Services, asked a very penetrating question: can transparency be measured? His question was intended to refer to transparency in companies and in countries. Financial audits, he said, were measures of compliance with the rules and practices of accounting, while country risk reports were generally about issues relating to political stability. Transparency, by contrast, was something else entirely. The more transparency, the greater the potential for business leaders and investors to see how things really operate inside companies or countries.

The discussion Jim Schiro and I had was not idle or academic. It was highly pragmatic. If you have the ability to peer deeply into an investment situation—a company or a market—the risk profile of that investment can suddenly change. Opacity—a term I coined and which Jim Schiro made fun of by calling it "Opa City," as if it were a place—is what obscures an investor's or business person's knowledge of what is taking place inside companies and countries. As a result, high levels of opacity equate with high levels of uncertainty and risk, the same way driving in the dark with weak headlights makes even familiar roads much more dangerous to navigate.

We decided to try to measure opacity since we could identify those things that obscure an investor's or businessperson's view. Those indicators were grouped into five categories—corruption, the way the legal system works, economic and enforcement policies, accounting standards and corporate governance, and regulation—which form the acronym CLEAR. Understanding the degree to which the view is obscured by these factors became a new way to examine risk, price it, manage it, and forecast where troubles might appear. Jim thought this work was worthy of PricewaterhouseCoopers support. Over the next several months, I put together a group of interested individuals within PricewaterhouseCoopers and outside the firm who wished to understand business risks better. Inside the firm, Alison Blair, Jermyn Brooks, Carlo Diflorio, Jill Hassan, Rocco Maggiotto, and William Daufinais were important contributors. Among those working on this project from the outside were Barry Herman, director of the United Nations economic survey unit; Shang-Jin Weifrom of the Brookings Institution and Harvard University; Daniel Kaufmann of the World Bank (who has adopted some of our metrics); Paolo Mauro and Vito Tanzi of the International Monetary Fund; Robert Klitgaard of the Rand Corporation; Jennifer McCoy at the Carter Center; and Jeffrey Garten and Susan Rose-Ackerman at Yale University. Among our advisers were President Jimmy Carter; Peter Eigen, chairman of Transparency International; and Frene Ginwala, speaker of the South African Parliament.

The Milken Institute, and Glenn Yago, became involved in the project in 2001. Among Glenn's team members working on the project were Senior Fellow James Barth and a research team consisting of Tom Hall, Cindi Li, Teresa Magula, Ed Phumiwasana, and Fang Rong.

Achieving acceptance for this work was not easy—at least at first. The Opacity Index and the way it defines, discusses, and manages risks is new. As so often occurs, new ideas often meet with opposition. A great deal of the opposition that arose proved to be constructive. As a result, we changed and adjusted concepts, altered methodologies, and shifted the way we created and weighted our ratings. Other forms of opposition were less helpful. And yet, the Opacity Index has gained currency.

Since my initial discussions with Jim Schiro, the Opacity Index has been put under the microscope. It has been peer-reviewed at MIT, defended and discussed at Wharton, and incorporated into research at the World Economic Forum. Business and financial journalists have also examined it. So far it has passed all of these tests.

Over the last few years, the Opacity Index and its related analysis tools have been used as part of investment screens by pension funds and intergovernmental lending agencies and employed by countries wishing to become more transparent. Companies have used it to make decisions with respect to plant and headquarters locations. Law firms, consulting firms, and other professional services firms have used it to council clients.

This book represents a major step forward in turning a simple idea into a new way of looking at risk. Its refinement and development have come about because of the help of a great many people, including especially Jacqueline Murphy, our editor at Harvard Business School Press, and Helen Rees, our indomitable agent. I remain grateful to all of them.

—Joel Kurtzman

Introduction

The Opacity Index offers a new concept of what matters in the global economy and a new system for rating and thinking about risk. The concept is deceptively simple and yet applies to large and small economic systems of varying degrees of complexity. Both companies and countries can benefit from this index. Mastering the concept, extensions, and applications of opacity provides business and government leaders with the ability to manage and classify risks and to accelerate growth.

What do we mean by *opacity*? It is simply the lack of clear, accurate, formal, clear-cut, and widely accepted practices in the broad arena where business, finance, and government meet. If the "intersection" of these forces is opaque, it can become a business bottleneck of enormous proportions, fraught with uncertainties and tremendous costs. Opacity is such an enormous (though rarely discussed) problem, it can retard the progress of globalization, slow down growth, and add a great many unanticipated costs to doing business.

The definition of opacity drills down yet one more level, splitting the factors that contribute to opacity into five categories:

- Level of *corruption*

- Effectiveness of *legal* systems

- Effectiveness of *enforcement* policies

- Transparency of *accounting*

- *Regulatory* quality and enforcement.

These five factors create a remarkably apt acronym: CLEAR.

This is a new concept, having only been published in a scholarly context in MIT's *Sloan Management Review*, and also as data without commentary in the *Economist* magazine.[1] We trust that our readers will look at it with curiosity—that they will want, in effect, to pick it up, to see how it works, and assess how it might help them with their concerns, whether they are in business and finance, government, or the world of nongovernmental organizations (NGOs). The opacity intersection—where commerce and business meet—is pivotal to how and where companies do business.

Certain values accompany the concept of opacity. The first of those values is that economic growth urgently matters for our world today, not only because shareholders have an understandable preference for growth and profitability but also because international peace and the decency of individual lives depend on economic progress.

The second value is that a reasonable level of transparency in economic systems is essential for sustained growth. There is good evidence that this is so. Countries that tolerate or even support an excess of opacity anywhere within the CLEAR factors are sacrificing something, and in some instances a very great deal. That "something" may be additional foreign direct investment or lower interest rates on the sovereign bonds they issue. Excessive opacity may also add to the sum of human suffering by making it more difficult to overcome entrenched poverty.

The third value underlying the Opacity Index is that the decisions and policies of businesses, governments, and NGOs can separately and interactively craft a global economy in which sufficient transparency emerges. Opacity is man-made. So, too, is transparency—it results from innumerable sensible and sometimes courageous decisions, and their implementation on a worldwide basis.

In this expanded and general release of the Opacity Index—
which now addresses some 90.3 percent of global GDP—and the
concepts behind it, you will find what amounts to a map of opacity—
and transparency—encompassing dozens of countries. Periodically,
the Opacity Index is updated, tested, and refreshed. Each time this is
done, opacity scores and costs are recalculated. Some of these calculations are updated quarterly, others annually, and some only every
few years. The point is, while opacity scores change, some change
more rapidly than others. The latest Opacity Indexes can always be
found at www.kurtzmangroup.com and at www.milkeninstitute.org.

The Opacity Index has been taken as good news in some countries and mixed or even unpleasant news in others. Some of the findings raise questions—they ask us, as researchers, businesspeople, or
government agents, to think and review. There are encouragements
and cautions: some findings are surprising and counterintuitive;
others reinforce standard views, although from a new vantage point.
This much the findings all have in common: they are intended to
help, to further recognition of the crucial role played by transparency in economic progress, and to support better decision making. Where there is unpleasant news, there is also an invitation to
plan and achieve realistic reforms that will improve that country's
economic health. And we might add that where there is pleasant news,
there is still almost always room for improvement. Every nation's economy is a work in progress and every company seeks to better understand its risks.

For businesses, the Opacity Index is a template for measuring
key aspects of a country's overall risk. It is a factor that belongs in
any calculation of expected rates of return, any decision about the
location of new facilities, and any assessment of the ease or difficulty
of ongoing operations in an indexed country.

For business, knowing a country's opacity—and the forces behind that score—contributes to better decision making along the following parameters:

- Better decisions regarding where to place regional headquarters as well as production, distribution, and marketing facilities

- Better understanding of hidden costs associated with different countries

- Better global merger and acquisition strategies

- Better understanding of the real cost of capital in different locations

- Better strategies for writing contracts and other legal agreements and indicating in which jurisdictions disputes should be resolved

- Better tools for assessing the growth of a market, the spending ability of the people, and the strength of the financial system

- Better ability to weigh overall global risks

- Better understanding of *hidden* costs (such as corruption) and risks (such as thefts of patents and lack of patent protections)

- Increased ability to run "what if" scenarios to determine optimum locations from a risk-management perspective

- Increased ability to weigh portfolio risks

- Increased ability to take the long-term view of markets

- Better insight into the reliability of corporate governance, regulation, and accounting standards

For governments, the Index offers new information that will support a wide range of positive actions, from clarification of legal, accounting, and regulatory systems to greater investment in anticorruption enforcement. As countries take action, their risk factors are likely to shift.

In some ways, we regard the Opacity Index as a lever for business and government, together with NGOs, to maintain control. If governments make positive changes, such as clarifying property rights, a country's score will be enhanced. Even more importantly, as rights are defined, businesses will take notice and countries formerly shunned by business enterprises will become attractive. Some of these countries—specifically Thailand, Taiwan, Korea, Israel, and Malaysia, which we call the "Edge countries"—have made positive changes over the years. They've clarified their laws, privatized sectors of their economies, and improved corporate reporting and governance. While not top-ranked, they provide businesses with a host of opportunities and they do so without huge hidden costs. They are relatively safe and far less risky than countries such as Brazil, Russia, India, and China (the "BRIC" countries, for short), with large markets but lax controls and high levels of corruption.

Whereas the BRIC countries have received large amounts of inbound investment due to their size and inexpensive labor, the Edge countries have also received investment, albeit in a quieter and, in some respects, more productive way.

What this shows is that actions taken by government affect business directly by turning a country with high-level opacity risks into an area that is safe for business. Korea is a case in point. In the late '90s, it was caught in a firestorm of problems due to the Asian currency meltdown and years of corrupt, nearly oligarchic rule. After the meltdown occurred (the so-called Asian Contagion), Korea began taking its opacity risks seriously and members of the government contacted us. Many of Korea's *chaebols*—government-sanctioned, family-controlled corporate empires—were broken up. Its laws were reformed along with its corporate governance and accounting rules. Corrupt officials and business leaders were sent to jail. While not rising to United Kingdom or Finnish levels of transparency, Korea made great strides. As a result, not only did its economy grow rapidly, but new foreign investment rushed in. Korea came out of Asia's problem period rapidly and has been growing quickly ever since.

For NGOs, the Index can provide relevant information. More importantly, however, it offers a fresh and unifying concept of the forces at work in global markets. Many NGOs wish to play a positive role globally by advising, lobbying, and protesting certain political and corporate behaviors. But until now, most of the information NGOs relied upon was anecdotal. The Opacity Index provides NGOs with a new tool with which they can compare behaviors in forty-eight countries—from workers' rights to shareholders' and debtors' rights. And, perhaps most importantly, since the Opacity Index is a snapshot taken in time, NGOs can now measure the extent of changes undertaken. Did a government really follow an NGO's advice? Or did it simply answer a criticism with promises and diversions? Before the advent of the Opacity Index, it was difficult to tell.

Measuring the *costs* of certain behaviors on a global basis, the Opacity Index does not engage in ethical or cultural commentary, nor does it finger-point. It is simply a tool to provide information, which can be taken up by all sides in explorations and controversies that touch on these issues.

In our own work, we have helped government policymakers and company leaders make use of our opacity data to increase the attractiveness of certain countries for investment and to lessen company risk. We have helped direct investors weigh and weight their portfolio risks and we have also endeavored to spread the word that some of businesses' biggest costs are hidden. We have helped make opacity data part of the corporate strategy and planning process and we have met and advised pension funds and other global investors. We have briefed corporate lawyers around the world. And finally, we have helped companies understand "what went wrong" when seemingly good investments failed to pay off.

In this book, we discuss opacity from several points of view—
with numbers, with anecdotes, and with short case studies—in an attempt to make the concept accessible. Our purpose in publishing this
book is to make available to the global community information on the
true costs and attendant risks of doing business in countries around
the world, and to offer policy makers a means of measuring the impact of the changes they propose. However, it must be added that we
are not neutral econometricians or businesspeople doing our jobs
from the sidelines. As researchers and as advisors to business and government, we have been committed for many years to the evolution of
transparent practices, and we remain so today. As rigorous in content
and form as we can make it, the Opacity Index is an argument for
transparency, which offers more favorable conditions for business and
the surest and shortest route to economic progress for nations.

The Opacity Index is independent. While some of the underlying
data that informs our work is produced by others—the World Bank,
for example—it is our analysis of that data that makes this work unique.
Even so, the Opacity Index correlates with several important indices. It
tracks closely with the World Economic Forum's Competitiveness Index, with the Heritage Foundation's Index of Economic Freedom, and
with the work of Transparency International. Taken together, this
means more than "we are not alone" in our work. It means that issues
like competitiveness, democracy, economic freedom, rule of law, and
access to capital correlate highly with transparency in business and
government, and with growth and the capacity to grow.

As you read this book, we hope that you ponder a number of
things. First, what you can see is far less risky than what you cannot
see. The clear light of day is the most powerful repellent to risk. As a
result, transparency makes a difference. Long ago, astronomers discovered "adaptive optics" that could analyze the distortion of light travel-
ing through the atmosphere and compensate for it in real time through
metrics. Atmospheric turbulence causes the romantic, but blurring,

"twinkle" that distorts observation. Economists and investors have not heretofore developed ways to counteract the financial and business counterparts to atmospheric turbulence of economic data. The Opacity Index enables the correction of those distortions and allows a glimpse into assessing the risks associated with them. By correcting the distortions systematically, we can see economic risks more clearly and understand how they are distributed.

Second, following from Peter Drucker, if you can't measure it, you can't manage it. Managing requires the ability to estimate and price the everyday risks of doing business. Opacity can be measured and therefore priced in a manner similar to the way pollution can be measured and its damage and abatement priced. Risks are not abstract; they are issues, events, and items with costs and consequences that can slow growth and wreak havoc within companies and countries. If companies understand their risks, not only will they be able to manage them, they will also be able to make better decisions.

By examining the contents of this book, we hope that people in business, government, and NGOs will begin to see the world differently, enabling them to craft better strategies, develop better tactics, and make better decisions about what really matters.

—Joel Kurtzman
   Glenn Yago
   Santa Monica, California

Chapter One

Everyday Risks of Going Global

A NUMBER OF YEARS AGO, a friend of ours relocated to Shanghai from Silicon Valley to introduce his United States–based computer networking company into the Chinese market. Everything seemed to go well at first until he learned that a Chinese company with which he had been working had stolen his company's proprietary software codes. Since his company's software was by far its most important and valuable asset, our friend brought a lawsuit against his Chinese competitor in the Chinese courts. Getting a date to have his company's case heard took quite some time and a few days before the case was to be heard, he was summoned to the judge's chambers to meet with the judge.

"Let's go for a walk," the judge said to our friend.

Not knowing what to expect, our friend went for the walk, during which the judge told him that if the case went to court, it was likely that one of the Chinese witnesses who had observed the theft of the software would "disappear." Without that witness, our friend's company would have a difficult time making its case. If the company still wanted to pursue its lawsuit, the judge said, other people were also likely to disappear. In the end, our friend's company would probably be asked to leave the country, according to the judge, though its software code would stay with the Chinese company that had stolen it.

"But my company's intellectual property has been taken without payment or permission," our friend protested.

"Then I suggest you try to settle your dispute with the Chinese company yourself, outside of the courts," the judge advised. "That's the better way to do it."

Ultimately, our friend had no choice but to allow his Chinese rivals to steal his company's code and it left a bitter taste in his mouth for years. But not only did it leave a bitter taste, the theft of these codes created a powerful rival to our friend's company. In China, and in other markets in Asia, stolen software codes have fueled the rise of competitors. Our friend's company is only one of several companies that have had similar experiences in China and elsewhere.

The moral of the story is clear: in countries with risks akin to China's—and there are many of them—the traditional ways in which companies assess those risks are flawed. Corruption, impaired legal systems, poor economic and enforcement policies, and flawed accounting standards are often overlooked even by the advisory firms that are hired to help a company "globalize." And yet, unenforced regulations—to pick just one example—are a far greater risk to companies than coups, revolutions, and even terrorism.

While this story about China may be extreme, it is true. And yet, in our interactions with analysts, fund mangers, CEOs, CFOs, direct-investment strategists, and even lawyers over the years, talk about this type of risk when they discuss opportunities resulting from globalization is rare. Tragically, in many countries, the risks and associated costs resulting from corruption and lack of legal recourse are common and not insignificant. In many cases those costs can be assessed in the billions of dollars.

As ardent proponents of globalization we have spent many years studying the way the business world works from many different perspectives. We have examined it as economists, researchers, consultants, and also as businessmen. A great deal of what we have learned people are not always eager to hear. The opportunities in many countries around the world are tremendous and any advice that suggests a cautionary approach to taking advantage of those opportunities can be viewed negatively. And yet, as we mentioned, we are ardent proponents of globalization. Both of us have lived, worked, and conducted business abroad. Both of us have been involved with governmental, intergovernmental, and nongovernmental organizations. Both of us have also provided advice to portfolio and direct investors, which has resulted in significant investments being made around the world. Neither one of us wants to slow the pace of growth or hamper globalization. And yet, we urge caution. It is a dangerous world out there.

The biggest problem we have had in making our points known—which is one of the reasons for writing this book—is what we call the "data point of one" problem. Many people we know have done remarkably well doing business in one or more dangerous or poorly rated countries. They have come out unscathed and sometimes even richer. Some of these people, who really should know better, have even said to us, as one former colleague once did, "I have done business in Hungary for twenty years and I never had a problem. Stop rating Hungary so low." To which we say—with some self-satisfaction—"you, dear friend, are a data point of one while we, on the other hand, have looked at statistics, mountains of raw data, and a myriad of transactions. Our data contradicts you."

For all those people who have done business globally and prospered, especially in areas we rate poorly, bravo and congratulations! Smart, shrewd, and/or lucky people often come out on top no matter what they do, no matter where they do it, no matter with whom.

When one of us was a young economist at the United Nations, Sir Brian Urquhart, an Undersecretary General, told a story about how he jumped out of an airplane over France during World War II, only to find that his parachute would not open. As luck would have it, he landed on a haystack which cushioned his fall. After six months in an army hospital, Sir Brian went on to do great things, including at the UN.

Even so, Sir Brian never advised people interested in skydiving to forgo the use of parachutes. He realized that while he was profoundly lucky, he was really only a data point of one. Most people falling through the air with a chute that won't open will proceed to the ground with an entirely different result. It is *those* people we worry about and those people for whom this book was written.

For people who might not have Sir Brian's luck, there is *process*—meticulous analysis, preparation, and planning. For people without Sir Brian's luck, there are statistically derived "likely" outcomes. From that information, scenarios can be generated and forecasts of potential costs can be produced. From that information, individuals within companies can run "what if" scenarios to determine how they will fare in different countries and under different conditions. To shed light on processes by which these analyses can be made is another purpose of our research and of this book.

Why We Wrote This Book

Our aim for this book is to help people understand and prepare for the everyday risks they might encounter when they do business around the world. In our view, understanding and "pricing" those risks is more important than ever. A great deal is at stake. For portfolio investors searching the world for returns, understanding risk differentials on a country by country basis can provide extra insight to help build winning portfolios. Our work, we believe, can also be of service to portfolio managers, particularly in the United States, who invest money for state and private pension funds. Pension funds, which we have advised, are often at the mercy of state legislatures that require them to screen their investments along a number of dimensions. The Opacity Index, which we will discuss, with its five CLEAR factors (corruption, the legal system, enforcement policy, accounting standards and governance, and regulation) satisfies many pension-fund screens.

For direct investors, the opacity work we do provides metrics by which investment decisions can be made. It also provides a better understanding of the real costs of doing business in one country versus another. For example, think of the recent case of the investor group Skye Ventures, which is suing Venezuela for the country's refusal to honor bonds purchased from the Banco de Desarrollo Agropecuario in the 1980s. Venezuela claims the bonds were fake, part of a fraudulent scheme involving corrupt government officials. As a result, they have no obligation to pay. Should Venezuela refuse to pay out, Skye Ventures may be liable for up to $6 billion to bondholders.[1] These are the real risks of investment abroad. Using the tools of opacity, companies like Skye Ventures can get a better understanding of the real return on investment they need in order to overcome the risks. When opacity risks are priced into the equation of doing business globally, companies often make different decisions about where to locate and with which foreign companies to form partnerships and joint ventures. They can also create strategies about where to settle disputes, should they arise, and where to locate their legal headquarters.

Table 1-1 summarizes our findings regarding opacity. It is arranged, as noted, by the CLEAR factors, which leads to an average opacity score, an overall ranking, and ultimately, to costs associated with each country's unique mix of risk factors. As you can see from the ratings in the table, not all countries are created equal. Even so, in our opacity work, we are not making judgments or saying one nation's behaviors are better than another's. Rather, we are simply suggesting, through our research, that one nation's practices are more cumbersome, more risky and ultimately more expensive than another's. We are also suggesting, as a result, that the added expenses and inefficiencies that come from high levels of opacity result in slower growth, less foreign direct investment, and shallower capital markets. Corruption, poor legal protections and enforcement, inadequate accounting standards and methods, and poor regulation have costs and act as multipliers to all other forms of risk.

TABLE 1-1

2005 opacity scores

	CLEAR FACTOR					Average opacity score	Overall rank
	Corruption	Legal system	Enforcement	Accounting	Regulation		
United Kingdom	16	2	20	20	12	14	1
Finland	3	11	24	37	9	17	2
Hong Kong	20	11	13	33	15	19	3
United States	25	20	28	20	10	21	4
Denmark	6	14	22	50	19	22	5
Netherlands	14	21	22	37	22	23	6
Canada	23	14	37	29	15	24	7
Australia	14	17	29	50	11	24	8
Austria	15	11	32	50	17	25	9
Ireland	34	18	26	37	10	25	10
Sweden	8	26	23	50	19	25	11
Japan	33	21	30	22	22	26	12
Belgium	27	24	32	37	14	27	13
Switzerland	15	27	23	50	22	27	14
Germany	23	14	30	37	32	27	15
Singapore	13	25	25	67	10	28	16
South Africa	47	33	28	33	17	32	17
Chile	32	25	32	43	27	32	18
Taiwan	40	34	23	40	28	33	19
Thailand	58	34	35	20	21	34	20
Malaysia	47	36	30	30	26	34	21
Israel	26	33	42	43	26	34	22

CLEAR FACTOR

	Corruption	Legal system	Enforcement	Accounting	Regulation	Average opacity score	Overall rank
South Korea	50	35	26	30	36	35	23
Spain	31	24	36	67	23	36	24
Hungary	48	34	32	50	24	38	25
Portugal	33	29	32	67	32	39	26
France	32	46	35	50	33	39	27
Greece	50	30	37	50	30	40	28
Brazil	44	49	32	40	35	40	29
Czech Republic	56	36	35	44	36	41	30
Colombia	51	63	44	29	21	42	31
Poland	63	38	54	40	20	43	32
Turkey	59	42	34	44	36	43	33
Mexico	58	61	38	33	25	43	34
Italy	49	34	47	62	25	44	35
Ecuador	59	61	42	25	29	44	36
Argentina	62	63	42	30	25	44	37
India	57	44	45	30	46	44	38
Pakistan	72	51	47	33	22	45	39
Russia	74	42	41	40	31	45	40
Egypt	61	39	44	40	51	47	41
China	65	39	37	56	43	48	42
Philippines	69	55	54	33	36	50	43
Venezuela	68	69	52	30	29	50	44
Saudi Arabia	66	34	32	60	69	52	45
Indonesia	70	52	83	22	50	56	46
Lebanon	76	60	65	44	42	58	47
Nigeria	73	67	49	60	49	60	48

It's one thing to invest in a country where corruption is rampant. It's quite another to invest in a country where it is not only rampant but there is no legal recourse when it occurs.

As we shall discuss later in this book, opacity slows growth. A quickly growing country like China, for example, could grow even more rapidly if it cleaned up its act. Not only that, but China, in particular, would grow in a more balanced way if its opacity levels were reduced. A sound knowledge of opacity can have a profound effect on the creation of new laws, processes, and procedures that regulate the intersection between government and business. The right decisions made at the right time—and then enforced!—will not only have an impact on growth, but an impact throughout society. Furthermore, the right rules properly enforced can dramatically increase the competitiveness of countries and can make them much more attractive to investors.

One more point regarding table 1-1: countries move around on it. They undertake new reforms or they replace good laws with ones that are worse. In some cases, scandals, which indicate hidden systemic problems, suddenly come to light. If China, for example, where only a small fraction of companies have outside financial audits, were to require companies to subject themselves to high-quality outside audits, its standing in the Index would be positively affected.

Such changes in ranking are not the case for only emerging-market countries. Since our first chart was released in 2001, the United States, for example, has fallen a number of places largely due to the accounting and business scandals occurring at Enron, World-Com, and Tyco. In addition, in some instances the remedy is as bad as the problem. The Sarbanes-Oxley Act of 2002, for example, has created higher levels of transparency, but in an expensive and heavy-handed manner which—for many businesses—has increased their level of uncertainty.[2] In market-based economies, where commerce abhors friction, overregulation is as onerous, risky, and expensive as underregulation. As a result, rather than increasing the standing of the United States, *Sarbanes-Oxley* appears to have diminished it on our Index. At the same time, the United Kingdom has risen on our Index due to enacting a set of intelligent, predictable, and inexpensive market and pension reforms in the 1990s in the wake of scandals and regulatory gaffs surrounding BCCI, an infamous and corrupt Pakistan-based bank, and Robert Maxwell, a British media baron who looted his own company's pension fund. As a result—and as our Index predicted—London is stealing business away from New York as European companies choose the United Kingdom over the United States as the preferred place to raise capital.

Our Ongoing Research Explorations

As we will explain in more detail in chapter 2, we have been interested in the topics in this book for many years. Together and individually, we have studied the world's capital markets and its markets for debt. We have looked at macro- and microeconomics from the standpoint of the country and the firm. We have mapped capital flows in numerous studies, books, and articles, as well as access to capital. We have testified before Congress and special committees.

But the specific research that now forms the basis of this book began in 1999, when we started to wonder whether interest rates around the world adequately reflected the level of risk in different countries. We also began to wonder about the effect of transparency on markets. Why, for example, is equity capital usually cheaper in the United States and in Britain than in Germany or Japan? Is it simply a function of the relative size of these global capital markets or are other forces at work? And what does this mean for business?

Our initial research was funded by PricewaterhouseCoopers, where one of us was a senior partner and the other consulted. To understand the cost of risk (rather than simply its magnitude), we brought together a number of outside researchers. Most importantly, the Milken Institute formally began to advise PricewaterhouseCoopers on these questions.

But along with that, we also put together a "brain trust." That brain trust included researchers from the Rand Corporation, Yale's School of Organizations, the United Nations, World Bank, the International Monetary Fund, and the Carter Center. Barry Herman, at the time chief economist at the United Nations, was extremely helpful to us, as was the economist Shang-Jin Wei, a student of the effects of corruption on business who has held positions at the IMF, World Bank, and the Brookings Institution.

As we developed our methodology, we presented our findings to senior Wharton faculty who were focusing on risk. In addition, we worked closely with Jennifer McCoy at the Carter Center and with President Carter, who advised us on our first report and introduced it to the world in early 2001, at a meeting at the Carter Center. In 2005, in a mutually agreeable manner, PricewaterhouseCoopers withdrew from our research effort and it became a joint project of the Kurtzman Group and the Milken Institute.

Since 1999, we have advised companies and governments on opacity risks and their costs. Mexico, in particular, has embraced our efforts and used our work in its endeavor to create greater levels of transparency at the interface between business and government. Other governments have also embraced this work, though quietly, while still others have chastised us for scoring them at levels they considered too low. A senior official in one Eastern European country, who advised us regarding the intricacies of his country's corruption issues and legal system inadequacies, told us that if he were in any way identified with our work his life would be in danger.

To make certain we were on the right track, we subjected our work to the utmost scrutiny. Within PricewaterhouseCoopers, we presented it to economists and researchers studying capital markets, interest rates, global and regional economics, and capital costs. After each presentation—some of which were quite heated—we made alterations in our approach and methodology. We also subjected this work to the intense scrutiny of the academic community, publishing an article in MIT's *Sloan Management Review*, a peer-reviewed journal.[3]

At present, we are more certain than ever that the work we have laid out in this book is new and useful. And it is gratifying to learn that the concept of opacity, as we first began to define it in 1999, is now taking hold in business and academic circles.

What Bolivia, Venezuela, and Brazil Can Teach

After more than eight years of research, in our view global companies face two distinct types of risks: large-scale, low-frequency risks and small-scale, high-frequency risks. Although the large-scale risks—earthquakes, wars, coups d'état, and major acts of terrorism—are front-page news, they are mercifully rare. In fact, it is their rarity that makes them newsworthy. Even so, it is the small-scale risks—corruption, fraudulent transactions, bribery, legal and regulatory laxities, unenforceable contracts, breaches of codes of conduct—that represent the real costs to business. These risks interfere with day-to-day business transactions, add to costs and liabilities, slow growth, and make the future even more difficult to predict.

Though low-frequency, high-impact political risks grab headlines, their real cost to business is usually small. Even the costs of nationalizations, which occur about once every decade and a half, are small. For example, Evo Morales, who became Bolivia's president in early 2006, announced he was nationalizing his country's oil and natural gas fields. Morales, whose party represents the country's coca growers, said "the time has come, the awaited day, a historic day in which Bolivia retakes absolute control of our natural resources."[4]

But Morales is not truly expropriating those resources, most of which are owned by Latin American energy concerns. Rather, he is forcing companies to renegotiate their contracts. True, this is onerous for the companies and represents a severing of existing contracts by the government. But Morales's actions may ultimately be declared unconstitutional, and therefore null and void, by Bolivia's constitutional court. Though little comfort, this at least indicates that Bolivia elected a populist authoritarian and not a despot. In addition, Morales's decree will still allow foreign investors to participate in Bolivia's oil and gas business, though on less rich terms. Under the Morales regime's new rules, foreign companies operating the largest gas fields will be able to keep only 18 percent of the gas they produce, down from as much as 50 percent, while companies operating the smaller gas fields will be able to keep more—as much as 40 percent.

Abrogating contracts has costs. Indeed, this low-frequency, high-impact risk cannot be wished away or glossed over. But fortunately, costly incidents like this are rare. Consider another case—that of Venezuela.[5] Though its populist president, Hugo Chavez, first elected in 1998, has professed solidarity with Cuban president Fidel Castro and with Evo Morales, and expressed antipathy toward the United States and especially President George W. Bush, he has so far done nothing to disrupt U.S. business interests in Venezuela besides make noise. Nor has Chavez cut off oil. Since Venezuela supplies the United States with only slightly less oil than Saudi Arabia, Chavez's "oil weapon" could prove formidable, if he ever decided to use it. Thankfully, he has not done so. Nor is it likely he ever will, despite predictions to the contrary by a number of political risk consultants. And why would he? If he were to stop selling oil to the United States, his own people would lose out. In the world's oil bazaar, one thing you don't want to do is drive your best customer away.

Fortunately for the United States and for business in general, like most anti-Western and anti–United States leaders, Chavez is much more bark than bite. For all his populist rhetoric—including threats to nationalize oil—Chavez has allowed U.S. businesses to operate in Venezuela.

Even so, Venezuela does have real risks that far outweigh any risks associated with the Chavez's threats against the United States. These risks are the high-frequency, low-impact risks of opacity. Venezuela scores at the bottom of the opacity barrel, in company with Saudi Arabia and the Philippines. For companies wanting to tap into Venezuela's market, beware—and not just of Chavez.

While Venezuela looks like an inexpensive place to do business when all traditional costs are tallied, such as labor, energy, raw materials, and telecommunications, it is actually a very expensive place to operate when the hidden costs of corruption, legal-system failings, and economic and enforcement risks are thrown in. Venezuela's population of twenty-four million has an average per capita income of about $7,000, allowing it to masquerade as an attractive, upper-level, emerging-market country. However, its corruption and other opacity risks function as a hidden tax on commerce, explaining why most of Venezuela's citizens live far below a middle-class norm, belying the statistical average.

While it is only possible to estimate the cost of corruption roughly, we believe Venezuela's overall opacity problems are equivalent to a hidden tax in excess of 70 percent on companies doing business there. Such a large hidden tax represents a powerful drag on growth and equitable distribution of wealth. If Venezuela were to clean up its act to the levels Finland observes, the economy would produce the same results as cutting taxes by about 70 percent. That much money put into the hands of Venezuela's poor and middle classes—and into the hands of its businesses and investors—would do far more to jump-start Venezuela's moribund but oil-rich economy than any of Chavez's plans for socialism with a Latin American face. It would also take an economy that few companies are brave (or brash) enough to venture into and make it inviting.

Farther south, in Brazil, Lula da Silva was first elected president on a pro-labor, Socialist ticket and then reelected on the same platform.

And yet, one of Lula's first actions in his first term was to appoint Henrique de Campos Meirelles to head Brazil's Central Bank. Meirelles, a Brazilian citizen, had been chief operating officer of Fleet Bank in Boston (now part of Bank of America), where he was responsible for making certain Brazil repaid its loans to his bank during that country's dark period in the 1980s. In the 1990s, before becoming COO, Meirelles led Fleet's Brazilian operations from São Paolo. Hardly a socialist, Meirelles was a tough-minded banker looking out for his firm's interests. And, while Brazil's organized labor, socialist dispossessed, and dissatisfied may have elected Lula, they put him in office to help Brazil develop its economic potential, not destroy it. For that reason, it is unlikely Lula would do anything to antagonize global business. Brazil needs long-term foreign investment and Lula knows it.

As a result, rather than taking over Brazil's banks, factories, foreign corporations and farms, Lula has been focusing his efforts on fighting inflation and luring new companies *into* Brazil. He's also championed Brazil's export products. Since his election, Lula—whom the *New York Times* continues to call a "leftist"—visited President Bush in Washington, which was reciprocated with a visit from Bush to Brasilia.[6]

Even so, like Venezuela, Brazil continues to be a highly corrupt place to do business, where many costs businesses must bear are kept out of sight. That said, at about 17 percent, Brazil's hidden tax is a bit better than Venezuela's. If Brazil were to clean up its act and raise its standards to Hong Kong levels, it too would surge ahead in growth while becoming an extremely attractive place for companies to invest.

To be sure, not all countries are as benignly quarrelsome as Bolivia, Venezuela, and Brazil. North Korea, Iran, Syria, and Sudan, among others, present governments and business with a host of very high-impact, very low-frequency problems to confront. North Korea and Iran are developing nuclear weapons, Syria is supporting Hezbollah and Sudan is in the midst of a civil war and is thought to be providing bases for units of Al Qaeda. Not surprisingly, all countries listed as terrorist havens or rogue states are also countries with high levels of opacity. But luckily, the vast majority of countries are not part of this tiny group.

Political Risk Consultants and Where We Differ

Most political risk consultants make money by warning their globalizing business clients about high-impact events, such as wars and nationalizations, which fortunately never seem to happen. Among the worst offenders are the insurance companies. While not exactly in the business of scuffing your shoes only to sell you a shine, they do tend to become alarmist in areas where they sell risk-management products.

For example, at the beginning of 2006, Aon, a large global insurance brokerage based in Chicago, alerted its clients to the fact that Latin America was becoming riskier due to what it called the "emergence of left-wing governments."[7] It further said that "companies doing business in Venezuela and Bolivia are facing higher taxes, revision of contracts and threatened expropriation of assets."[8] What's interesting is that in our taxonomy of risk, which we describe in detail later on, only expropriation—often called nationalization—is a low-frequency, high-impact problem. We define it that way because the expropriation of a business investment or business asset usually means a company is out of business. But Aon's other worries, higher taxes and contract revisions, are exactly the kind of problems we define as low-impact, high-frequency. Why do we put them in that category? Neither higher taxes nor a revised contract will put you out of business. But what they will do is drive up costs. Having tools that forecast the imminence of these problems is vital to a company's long-term health.

In emerging-market countries—especially in Latin America—expropriations (or nationalizations) may be on Aon's worry list, but they are really not topics that should keep a run-of-the-mill, law-abiding CEO up at night. At least not any more. Despite the leftward tilt of Latin America, the last large-scale nationalization took place in Mexico in 1982, when the government took over the banks.[9] Also in 1982, France nationalized a mergers and acquisitions advisory firm owned by a Rothschild bank. Before that, in 1969, India also nationalized its banks.

What these incidents show is that large-scale nationalizations and expropriations are really astonishingly rare. Given the power they have at their disposal, most governments exhibit a high level of restraint when it comes to intervening in the economy. In fact, for at least twenty years, governments of all political stripes and in all regions have been selling off the properties they own, not nationalizing them. In our view, companies have no doubt paid out more money to political risk consultants and insurers over the last twenty years than they have lost from nationalizations.

Judgment Versus the Numbers

We have nothing against a group of former foreign services officers, academics, and spies getting together over a glass of scotch to talk about a country's prospects. That type of discussion is always interesting. Sometimes it is even right. For most political risk consultants, that is the extent of their methodology.

But when it comes to the science of prediction, it takes masses of people all focusing on the same issue to produce anything of value. Prediction markets work by aggregating thousands of perspectives about a topic into a single point of view, in the same way that investors combine their opinions about a country's prospects in the movement of the market. But for prediction markets to work, thousands of people need to play the game and the questions need to be clearly stated.

With firms, organizations, or agencies that utilize only a handful of experts, the chances of those experts figuring out a country's real risks are remote. Luckily for them, as we have already stated, high-impact events are rare. As a result, the aforementioned group of practioners will be right more than wrong if they advise that nothing on the macro level is likely to happen. Like a stopped clock that is right once a day, this approach to global risk can also be right by default.

But as the world has learned rather painfully, CIA experts sitting in offices and cubicles in Langley, Virginia, looked at the tea leaves regarding Iraq and saw weapons of mass destruction that were not there. By contrast, weapons inspectors who actually wandered around Iraq reported to Washington and the UN that there were no weapons of mass destruction.[10] For reasons about which we can only speculate, public opinion and government policy sided with the group at Langley, rather than with those whose boots were filled with sand.

Businesses, if they are to globalize successfully, need to make decisions based on fact, not fear, politics, or opinion. The sole purpose of a company's leadership—if we understand business correctly—is to make good decisions. You cannot do that without the right kind of inputs. Once a company is cognizant of CLEAR and understands how one country compares with another, they can make good decisions about where to invest their own or their shareholders' or investors' money. But even more importantly, once they have access to real information about the way a country's economy works, they can decide *how* to invest that money.

War, Terrorism, and Other Problems

Rather than presenting businesses with large costs, war and terrorism tend to instead have cooling effects on business in a general sense. True, companies like Cantor Fitzgerald and others that were located in New York's World Trade Center sustained expensive business losses, in addition to devastating human losses, due to the 9/11 attack. But research conducted by the Milken Institute suggests that the major effects of a terrorist incident, such as those that occurred in New York, Madrid, Bali, and London, are that they put new investment on hold.[11] In each of these countries, the financial markets faltered in the aftermath of the attack. However, in each case, the markets recovered once the immediate threat had passed.

Aside from areas where terrorism is a proxy for war—Iraq, Israel, Afghanistan, and perhaps Pakistan—the frequency with which these heinous acts have occurred has been rare. One reason why large-scale terrorist events are low-frequency is their complexity. The events of 9/11 required years of reconnaissance, planning, and training, which had to happen in secrecy at a number of training centers and bases around the world. Recruiting teams of suicide hijackers who spoke English, were technologically adept, and were capable of blending in with U.S., British, and German society without arousing suspicion did not come without complications. How easy could it have been to find people willing to die in suicide missions *who were also capable of studying at American flying schools without being detected?* And how easy could it have been to find people who were agreeable to suicide missions and to training at U.S. flight schools but were also capable of living undetected in the United States for years without losing any of their zeal?

The point is that the more complex the operation, the more time it will take to execute. The more time it takes to execute, the more vulnerable it will be to detection. For that reason, the bigger the impact, the more rarely it occurs.

Crack teams of terrorists are likely to be few in number and this is a very big world. While it is possible that someday a team will emerge with sufficient weaponry to devastate a city, we would all be unwise to confuse worry with any real evidence of threat. Because something *can* happen, it does not mean it will happen. And while we must be vigilant, we also must be clear-headed and wise. The main impact of terrorism is fear, not devastation.

We also must be wary of the CNN or BBC effect, which is to say that when an event happens in a country and CNN or the BBC covers it, the result of that coverage is to intensify the perception of threat. The media in general tend to take a single—perhaps even isolated—incident and generalize it. In large part, this is a function of the technology and the news. A camera, after all, only shows one tiny area at a time. If a bomb goes off and the camera follows soon after, it is hard not to feel that the country where the incident occurred is under siege. And yet, in most parts of the world countries are safe, whereas a few neighborhoods or even towns might be very dangerous.

We are not being Pollyannaish, only realistic. The world *in general* is a far less dangerous place that many of us think. As a result, the cost of war for businesses is mostly the cost that comes from vacating a dangerous region and hiring local intermediaries to fill in the gaps. Iraqis and Afghanis still buy products from global firms; they just buy them through local intermediaries usually at higher costs. If the economists are right, and we believe they are, higher prices decrease sales volume, but they do not necessarily suspend it. Wars have chilling effects but they don't end business altogether.

It may be argued that high opacity *contributes* to terrorism and war. Endemic corruption, then, is an international security problem. For example, there are few people who would dispute the fact that Kenya is one of the most corrupt countries in the world. Dr. Kim Howells, a Foreign Office Minister from Britain, argued on his visit to the country in late 2006, that Kenya is "wide open" for drug cartels and terrorists.[12] Because of this corruption, he said, terrorists and drug traffickers can take advantage of what they perceive to be a weak system to conduct their illegal activities. He added that an apparent surge in Al Qaeda activity in neighboring Somalia last year had heightened the risk to Kenya and had big implications for regional and international security. High opacity and antisocial behavior of all types are linked.

Small-Scale Risks Are Big

Though high-impact, low-frequency risks garner the world's attention, small-scale, high-frequency risks are what cost it money. The direct costs of corruption—one of the five types of high-frequency, low-impact risks that we study—are massive. According to a 2003 research study by the World Bank, corruption costs the world $1.5 trillion a year—only slightly less than the entire economic output of the Chinese economy or about 5 percent of the world's gross domestic product.[13] That's a lot of money businesses and individuals let slip through the cracks and into the pockets of thieves working in governments around the world.

It is bad enough that $1.5 trillion ends up being used so unproductively. But worse yet, a huge portion of it gets siphoned off in the form of bribes. What is a bribe? It is a payment you are forced to make to get something done that you already paid for, either through taxes or fees. If you pay a government office $20 to obtain a building permit, but have to pay a government official $200 to "facilitate" the processing of that permit, you are paying two times for the same thing. But in high-corruption countries, you pay twice everywhere. You pay an unloading tax for cement, *plus* a fee to the police to let you unload; you pay an export tax; *plus* a fee to the harbormaster to let your cargo leave the port; you pay an entrance tax, *plus* a fee to have your passport stamped. Countries with high levels of corruption mean you pay double—at least—for everything. And since these second payments are not logged into the country's official statistics, this contributes to chronic underestimating of the true costs of doing business around the world.

Corruption is not evenly distributed around the world. Our research shows that some countries, like Denmark, are as clean as a new winter snow. Others, like China, Nigeria, Brazil, Indonesia, Lebanon, and Russia, are places where very little gets done without someone's palm getting greased. In some countries, the receipt of payments by corrupt government officials is perhaps the most efficient activity those government officials do. Without those payments, many corrupt officials simply stop or slow progress. They are nothing more than parasites.

The burden of corruption has a greater negative impact on the world's emerging market countries than on the world's developed nations. In our research, as will be shown, corruption acts as a brake—an added tax, if you will—on economic development and growth. Even rapidly growing countries like China would grow faster still if their high levels of corruption were eliminated.

Show Us the Money

The World Bank estimates that $30 billion in African development assistance has been stolen from the people and institutions for which it was intended. The money, according to the Bank, was earmarked for everything from food to the purchase of medical goods, from roads to bridges, from water wells to pipelines, from pesticides to seeds. According to researchers, much of that money now resides in bank accounts in rich countries like Switzerland where it is kept safe for the people who stole it.

One Asian country—the Bank preferred not to name which one—has "lost" $48 billion to corruption over the last twenty years. During that same twenty-year period, the unnamed country's foreign debt increased to $40.8 billion. Money earmarked for the poor went instead to corrupt officials. The debt was loaded on the backs of its poor.

Though widespread in the poorest countries of the world, the so-called developed world is not immune to corruption. A study conducted in 1999 and presented at a United Nations conference estimated that one North American city—it did not say which one—spent $1.5 billion a year collecting and managing its garbage, with about $330 million a year siphoned off by organized crime. While that may be good news for a mob boss and his crew, it's bad news for taxpayers and business owners The high cost of corruption—wherever it occurs—discourages investments. Though pervasive, corrupt practices are certainly not legal. In fact, under the United States' Foreign Corrupt Practices Act, agreeing to pay bribes can result in jail sentences for executives.[14]

Reputation and Shareholder Value

Other high-frequency, low-impact risks can create big costs for business. A company that works with suppliers that flaunt child labor or environmental laws can find itself in costly trouble. But in many instances, companies get into trouble not only when far-away suppliers thwart laws and regulatory strictures, but simply when they go against nonbinding, extra-legal codes of conduct. These nonbinding codes are often highly specific to industries. Toymakers and shoe companies have developed their own set of criteria for working with manufacturers in emerging markets.

Global, regional, and local nongovernmental organizations (NGOs), such as Greenpeace, the Rainforest Action Network, and European Partners for the Environment, are increasingly sophisticated and powerful. Many of them are staffed with people with advanced degrees and many have links to political parties and labor unions. In France, major antiglobalization groups like Attac are not just connected to its political parties and unions, but also to the media. Their strikes against certain brands, like McDonald's, do not go unnoticed. Rather, they are covered in detail by a semicaptive press.

Many of these NGOs have taken it upon themselves to become "watchdogs" in countries where rules are lacking or poorly enforced. A demonstration by an NGO is not something political risk firms pay much attention to because, while the provocation may have occurred in the developing world, the protests are often carried out in the headquarters country, near the investment community and—of course—the media.

Because of the interplay between codes of conduct and NGOs-as-watchdogs, Nike, Nestlé, Royal Dutch Shell, Wal-Mart, and others have sustained billions of dollars of losses in shareholder value as well as losses to their reputations. Wal-Mart's reputation is under assault from NGO groups for its labor practices in places as diverse as California and China, even though the giant retailer has done nothing illegal. The protests were staged because these NGOs feel Wal-Mart suppliers did not adhere strongly enough to a set of nonbinding, extra-legal codes of conduct governing supplier labor practices. To deal with these pressures, Wal-Mart now has more than one thousand inspectors who visit suppliers and has created a new position to oversee these efforts. In addition, it has launched a PR and advertising offensive. The cost to Wal-Mart of doing this is not insignificant.

Nike—one of the world's most recognizable brands—is another company that lost billions of dollars in shareholder value due to the way one of its independent suppliers in Indonesia treated its younger workers. Even though the supplier was doing nothing illegal under Indonesian law, its business practices became big news when NGOs began talking to the media.

Nestlé also lost billions in value—and is still subject to protests and taunts from NGOs, especially in Europe—for the way it marketed its infant formula in the developing world over two decades ago. More recently, Nestlé has come under attack for the practices of the farmers and wholesalers from which it buys chocolate and coffee in South America and Africa. These farmers do not work for Nestlé, but Nestlé bears the brunt of the NGOs opprobrium. As one NGO leader told us, "we know Nestlé is not responsible for the farmers' and middlemen's practices. But we also know if we pressure Nestlé, it will put pressure on those farmers to change their ways."

Shell has also been subject to protests throughout Europe for doing business in Nigeria and has even been accused erroneously of murder by some NGO groups. The cost to Shell was not only in shareholder value, but also in damage to its reputation. Since premium brands like Shell can charge premium prices, damage to that brand costs money, directly and indirectly. When Shell faced a real scandal in 2002 for inaccurately accounting for its petroleum reserves, it had to convince the world this error was a one-time event and not a part of a broader pattern encompassing its Nigerian operations. With the loss of reputation capital, the public assumes a company is guilty at the outset—a presumption that a company must then work hard to disprove. For a company to prove itself innocent in its customers' and investors' eyes, heavy spending on marketing, PR, and advertising is typically required.

Economic Development

Growth and development are among the most studied topics in economics, primarily because several questions remain unanswered: What causes growth? Will all nations reach the same level of development (convergence)? What does it mean for a country to go from "undeveloped" to "developing" and finally "developed" status?

Broadly speaking, development should encompass the social, environmental, structural, human, and governance characteristics of a nation, not just the economic and financial factors. However, for operational and analytical purposes, the main criterion for classifying economies is gross national income (GNI) per capita (previously referred to as gross national product). Based on its GNI per capita, every economy can be classified as either low-income, middle-income, or high-income. Low-income and middle-income economies are generally referred to as developing economies. The classification is not intended to imply that all economies in a group are experiencing similar development or that other economies have reached a final stage of development. However, overall prosperity and human progress depend on long-term growth which can be measured by average per capita income and its rate of accumulation. To this end, there are two primary areas of development strategies:

1. Promoting economic opportunities through equitable growth, better access to markets, and expanded assets

2. Enhancing security by preventing and managing economy-wide shocks and providing mechanisms to reduce the sources of vulnerability

Recent development strategies emphasize the particular importance of financial markets for building and maintaining robust and stable economies. In the context of this view of development, opacity helps us understand the systemic factors that could prevent a country from "making it"—that is, moving into the developed nation category. The topic parallels concerns about state failures by looking at financial market failures. In table 1-2, we have identified twenty-six nations, among the poorest on the planet, which have received no private external financing in nearly thirty years. Overriding problems in opacity have prevented stable financial markets from developing in these countries.

Foreign Direct Investment (FDI) has been growing rapidly, at a pace far exceeding the growth in international trade. Thus, a full understanding of the relationship between trade in goods and FDI is important for obtaining a complete picture of the extent and sources of the economic connections between two countries (international linkages). Often, the amount of international trade undertaken by a country serves as a proxy for its level of openness or as a measure of the linkages between two countries. However, the central FDI question is whether a country's level of opacity increases or decreases its volume of trade. The Opacity Index helps us understand unseen barriers to trade and investment and the costs associated with these barriers when they occur.

TABLE 1-2

Low-income countries receiving no private, long-term, nonguaranteed external credit (1970–1999)

Country	2000 population (in thousands)
Benin	6,284
Burkina Faso	11,274
Burundi	6,807
Central African Republic	3,597
Chad	7,694
Comoros	558
Congo, Democratic Republic	51,390
Congo, Republic	2,936
Ethiopia	64,298
Gambia	1,286
Guinea	7,418
Guinea-Bissau	1,207
Haiti	7,959
Lao, PDR	5,216
Lesotho	2,154
Liberia	3,130
Madagascar	15,423
Mali	10,840
Mauritania	2,669
Myanmar	45,611
Nepal	23,920
Rwanda	8,508
Sierra Leone	5,031
Somalia	9,711
Togo	4,670
Uganda	22,063

Source: World Bank, World Development Indicators, 2001.

Another key reason for understanding these linkages arose in the aftermath of the currency and financial crises of the 1990s. If capital inflows to a country are large and abruptly change course, important real consequences can ensue. In many countries, reversals in foreign capital availability can lead to a redistribution of productive factors within a country. The availability of investment funds and new physical capital can have important consequences for the future structure of a country's trade and the welfare of its citizens.

What does this mean? In practice—and with only a handful of exceptions—the higher the opacity, the greater the drag on growth, trade, and investment. In addition, higher levels of opacity mean higher overall (but often hidden) costs structures, greater levels of risk, and higher capital costs. High-opacity environments like India may have tremendous long-term business potential, but they are not business friendly and they are *always* more expensive places to do business than they seem at first glance.

The Real Opacity Risks

To better understand, manage, and predict opacity risks on a country-by-country basis, we divided them into five categories:

- Level of *corruption*

- Effectiveness of *legal* systems

- Effectiveness of *enforcement* policies

- Transparency of *accounting* and corporate governance standards

- *Regulatory* quality and enforcement.

These five factors make up the acronym CLEAR.

After conducting several thousand interviews around the world under the auspices of PricewaterhouseCoopers, we came to the conclusion that the real risks business face are the ones associated with the five CLEAR factors: level of corruption; effectiveness of legal systems; effectiveness of enforcement policies; transparency of accounting and corporate governance standards; and regulatory quality and enforcement. In those interviews, we asked analysts, CFOs, accountants, business leaders, and a number of academics to give us their views regarding risks. Our interviews confirmed which risks matter most to global businesses: those that occur every day. As a result, we then spent years creating our Opacity Index, as a way to calculate the impact of those factors.

As a concept, CLEAR is related to what economists and social scientists call "social capital," adapted to a business concept. Social capital refers to the institutional arrangements that enable commercial and economic transactions to occur with a reasonable certainty and with high levels of trust between the parties. Positive social capital allows businesspeople to feel secure that their economic exchanges are fair and that rules will be enforced equitably if a problem occurs. In addition, it posits that arbitrary actions—a breached contract, for example—will be rare and that when they happen there will be consequences.

Corruption, as already discussed, represents an enormous cost to businesses around the world. However, corruption is really part of a larger continuum of behaviors. Imagine a horizontal line from left to right with a point at the center. A civil servant who will not act without being paid bribes is at the extreme left of this continuum. A civil servant who will act without payment for relatives and friends, but who charges strangers and foreign businesses a "facilitation fee" to do routine work is a bit closer to the center. A civil servant who is inefficient and bored, but who does not take bribes, is at about the middle of the continuum. A civil servant who is efficient, helpful, quick, and charges no "fees" is to the right of center along the continuum. Finally, an automated system whereby one obtains a permit online and pays for it online—as they do in Australia, Singapore, Britain, and other countries—is at the extreme right of the continuum. At that far right point, interactions with the government are straightforward and traceable. Each payment goes where it is intended while receipts and permits can be printed out as the transaction is made. There are no favors granted outside the rules or law.

One side of the continuum represents high added costs with lots of friction—facilitation payments may engender other such payments and, rather than speed up the process, may in fact slow it down. And there is always the possibility that the bribe payer gets arrested along with the bribe taker. At the other end of the continuum everything takes place quickly and without friction. One end is expensive, the other cheap. One end is highly opaque, the other transparent.

Each day, global businesses conduct hundreds of millions of transactions that fall somewhere along this continuum. Sometimes they are with governments, but these same continuums exist when business is conducted entirely within the so-called private sector. We know of an in-house advertising director at a major global airline, for instance, who required the advertising agency with which he did business to secretly pay his country club dues if the agency wanted to win work from the airline. Those fees were not cheap and other advertising agencies, unaware of the secret deal, spent hours bidding unsuccessfully for work they could never win.

The costs, risks, and friction from that type of transaction were far higher than either side admitted or carried on its books. Not only that, but those transactions took time, effort, and ingenuity to hide. If this hidden arrangement was uncovered through an investigation in the United States, the CEO and perhaps the head of the audit committee of the board of directors could go to jail under provisions of the Sarbanes-Oxley legislation. The airline and the advertising agencies were moderately far along the left side of the continuum.

Each of the five CLEAR factors operates along similar continuums. Because we conceive of them as continuums, we are able to measure where each country lies on a scale, and thus make more accurate comparisons between countries. By viewing the five issues as behaviors—not crimes—and attaching no moral judgments, we can skirt the argument that "we do it in our country this way while you do it in your country that way. It's simply our custom." Our research shows that the cheapest and most efficient behaviors are those that are the most transparent.

To measure opacity and construct our continuums, we analyze about seventy variables per country. These include seemingly minor points, such as the number of procedures it takes to get a grievance heard in court (the fewer the better), whether creditors can participate in bankruptcy proceedings (if they can't, that puts investment money at risk), the number of credit rating agencies operating in the country (the more the better, and the more independent they are, better still), whether banks are required to have independent auditors, whether property rights are clearly defined, and so on. These so-called minor points connect with the larger ones, like corruption.

Understanding each CLEAR factor can help companies avoid problem countries or create strategies to protect themselves if they have no choice but to invest in highly opaque areas. In countries with poorly functioning legal systems, for example, companies can still do business there by entering into contracts that are mediated in nearby countries with better legal scores. In countries where accounting standards are poor, agreements can be made to use international accounting standards.

After assessing the magnitude of these business risks, we then examined our data to get an appreciation of opacity's cost. What is worrisome is that a number of countries that present businesses with high levels of opacity risks—China, India, and Russia, in particular—are attracting the lion's share of the world's investment capital. China alone attracted more than $54 billion of foreign investment capital in 2005. Companies that ignore these risks do so at their own peril. While these countries may be politically stable, they are not financially safe.

Opacity is not just a problem for businesses; it is a problem for governments. As we've said, high-frequency, low-impact risks operate as a hidden tax. But unlike most taxes that are designed to provide something of value in return for the money they take, the "opacity tax" results in higher costs and less-efficient procedures. Some countries, like Mexico, which are making attempts to clean up their acts, have put the Opacity Index on their government Web sites. Other countries have publicly decried our efforts to shed light on their problems, while privately telling us to continue with our work. "We need to clean things up," one Minister told us. "But we sometimes need external pressure in order to do so."

If countries became less opaque, companies doing business there would receive the economic equivalent of a tax cut without any loss of income to the country's treasury. We have calculated the value of that "tax-cut equivalent" for each of the countries we studied and found it significant.

Companies need to understand that in order to take advantage of global markets and global labor, they must comprehend their risks. Whereas most companies are adequately informed about risks that almost never occur, they fall short when it comes to protecting themselves against those small and costly problems that happen every day. Companies must spend more time reading legal codes and less time listening to what the political risk consultants say.

What Opacity Does and Doesn't Measure

So what does the Opacity Index do? Risks vary on a country by country basis, most people agree. But political analysts cannot tell you the price of a future event, they can only tell its likelihood.

What we do, however, is create what we call a "proxy for price." In other words, if country X is a risky place, we attempt to price that risk. An opacity score of 22—1 point above the United States—means a company needs to get a return of 24.2 basis points (0.24 percent) above the benchmark United States in order to justify that investment. If a company does business in the United Kingdom, for example, it would need less of a return than in the United States—about 169 basis points less (1.69 percent)—because of the efficiency, transparency, and effectiveness with which business is transacted in the United Kingdom. In addition, because less goes wrong in the United Kingdom, vis-à-vis the United States (especially with respect to legal issues), the United Kingdom's long-term risk profile is better, ultimately, and less costly. We can see this play out in practice. The American capital markets, while still the world's largest, are rapidly losing business to markets in the UK. Investors, with many billions of dollars at stake, prefer the transparency of London to the relative murkiness of New York.

The Opacity Index works—we've tested it in practice—for a simple reason. According to the Efficient Market Hypothesis, prices are summaries of everything we know about a *thing*, such as a bond, stock, currency, car, at any given point in time. We therefore designed our Opacity Index to create the moral equivalent of a price. The information we analyze produces a number. That number, we believe, is a summary of everything we know about the way business is conducted in a country at any given time.

The Countries We Cover

The countries we covered in our research are extremely diverse. They include a number of mature industrial countries (both OECD and non-OECD), the majority of larger emerging market countries, a number of developing countries, and several Heavily Indebted Poor Countries (a term borrowed from the World Bank).

While these countries are comparable and even identical in some respects (all, for example, have one vote in the United Nations General Assembly), comparisons between countries of extremely divergent economic size and complexity can be misleading. In the economies of nations, size correlates with complexity. An application of Metcalfe's Law concerning networks sheds light here: just as a network becomes exponentially more complex and more valuable to all participants as more nodes are added to it, so too an economy becomes more complex and can generate greater value as more economic transactions are added to it. For example, comparing Botswana, a very transparent country, to the United States, another transparent county, is like comparing a local 7-11 to Wal-Mart. Although they do have things in common, level of complexity is not one of them.

Developed for the first release of our data in 2001, at the Carter Center and later refined many times, the metrics underlying the Opacity Index are still quite new. Our working definition of opacity, as noted earlier, is "lack of clear, accurate, formal, clear-cut, and widely accepted practices." The Index measures opacity by calculating each of the five CLEAR factors separately and aggregating those scores into a single composite opacity score for each country studied.

No country is likely to be completely transparent. There may be corruption in government bureaucracy that allows bribery or favoritism. The laws governing contracts or property rights may be unclear, conflicting, incomplete, or partially unenforced. Economic and enforcement policies—fiscal, monetary, and tax-related—may be vague or change unpredictably. Accounting standards may be weak, inconsistent, conceptually flawed, or unenforced, thus making it difficult to obtain accurate financial data. Business regulations may be unclear, inconsistent, or irregularly applied. The greater the opacity in any of these distinct (although often interacting) areas, the greater the adverse impact on the development or maintenance of broad, deep, liquid, well-functioning financial markets. Markets matching this description are clearly essential if funds are to be allocated efficiently from savers to investors, within and across national borders.

The Opacity Index is a new contribution to a current of research that has been progressing for some years. Researchers, for example, have examined the impact of corruption on economic growth and development and the relationship between macroeconomic transparency and the likelihood of financial crises. They have also considered the extent to which incomplete financial disclosure by banks may impede the ability of investors and regulators to take actions that would reduce the likelihood and associated costs of bank failures. Conversely, they have considered whether incomplete disclosure may enable bank managers to take actions that decrease the bank's viability or profitability or both.

How Opacity Adds Hidden Costs to Business

Opacity can lead to a situation that economists like Noble Laureate Joseph Stiglitz call "asymmetric information" flows, in which highly opaque firms or companies possess inside private information about their financial and business fundamentals that is not available to outside investors. Depending on how widespread, this circumstance can reduce investment in companies or countries. Why put money in a company if only its management understands its true health and makes business decisions based on proprietary "inside" information? The purpose of financial reporting—at least as it is defined in most developed countries—is to create a level playing field where all investors have access to a company's financial information at the same time. The Enron situation, wherein a tiny group of people knew the company's real financial condition and sold their holdings without disclosing the company's true condition, is a case in point. Though in the short term this small group prospered, in the longer term the company collapsed and brought down much of the wider market as it fell. The crimes at Enron were numerous, but in the end, the fall of that company was brought about by its opacity—a small group of people hiding financial information that the investment community needed to know.

Around the world, information asymmetries akin to Enron's have been linked by research to an increased cost of capital for firms in opaque countries, as well as to an increase in the bid-offer spreads on securities. In the first instance, investors demand a risk premium on their investments to compensate for uncertainty about a company's fundamental soundness. In the second instance, the presence in opaque financial markets of traders with private information about firms introduces market "distortions." What this means is that when investors are unable to distinguish between traders with private information and those without it, market makers must charge a premium to *all* traders to offset the expected losses they will suffer on deals made with individuals possessing private information. Greater opacity can therefore lower the amount of investment in an economy and decrease the efficiency of financial markets in allocating resources while, at the same time, increasing how much capital costs.

Research also indicates that, to the extent that opacity inhibits the ability of corporate governance systems to minimize what are technically called "agency costs," it represents an extra cost to companies when raising external funds in the markets and even from banks. Agency costs include the due diligence and monitoring costs incurred by bankers and investors when they have to ensure that managers are actually using the borrowed funds as stated. These costs add up and also contribute to a country's (and a company's) hidden opacity costs.

Deriving Opacity Index Ratings

Concerning the five CLEAR factors—corruption, legal opacity, enforcement opacity, accounting opacity, and regulatory opacity—there is every reason to believe that each negatively affects the development and efficient functioning of financial systems and thereby retards economic growth and development. There are no fully demonstrated reasons to believe that any one of these factors is more important than another. Therefore, our research has included inquiries about each of the five areas of potential opacity, and the responses in each area were weighted equally to generate a quantitative measure and thereafter a rating.

Several questions probed the extent and depth of perceived corruption and sought to gauge perceptions of its effect on the cost of capital. Corruption can adversely affect the cost of capital insofar as otherwise productive firms are crowded out of financial markets by politically connected or covertly favored firms. The allocation of capital in such situations would not reflect fundamental economic factors.

To determine the effects of legal opacity, we examined issues of shareholder protection, the predictability of the judicial system, and the enforcement of laws, regulations, and property rights. These questions enable an assessment of the influence of these factors on financial markets.

We attempted to measure economic and enforcement opacity through questions addressing the predictability of government policy as reflected in fiscal, monetary, and foreign exchange policies. Prior research supports the view that capricious and arbitrary government policy making in such areas increases the risk premium that firms and countries must pay when seeking capital. More generally, such policy actions impede the efficient functioning of financial markets.

Accounting opacity was addressed by questions concerning disclosure standards and access to information about publicly traded corporations. We assumed that firms that disclose more information are more attractive to investors because the relative risks of investing in those companies are more fully revealed. Firms that reveal more information about their fundamentals reduce what is technically called the "information costs" of investing in them.

Regulatory opacity, the fifth focus of our research, was addressed by asking questions concerning the presence or absence of clearly established rules for changing and consistently applying regulatory rules and procedures.

Each type of CLEAR score, and the Opacity Index itself, can range in value from 1 to 100. The best possible score is a 1, which a country would receive if all respondents and data points identified uniformly, perfectly transparent conditions. The worst possible score is a 100, indicating that all respondents and data points identified uniformly, perfectly opaque conditions.

Chapter Two

The Costs of Opacity

SUCCESSFUL GLOBALIZATION requires understanding more than investment costs. A business must thor-
oughly grasp the everyday risks and additional expenses so often
overlooked. Although the world is a big, sometimes dangerous, and
often expensive place, when going global, business leaders rarely
assess the small-scale, high-frequency risks related to opacity, leading to unexpected and sometimes exorbitant costs.

In 2005, according to a study of CEOs by Pricewaterhouse-
Coopers, a prevalent concern among CEOs was their inability to
really understand in depth what was going on inside their far-flung
companies.[1] In fact, while attempting to create meaningful country
rankings for the Opacity Index using survey data, we came to an
important conclusion: business leaders, ranging from CFOs and
CEOs to analysts and accountants, rarely understand business conditions in any detail in countries other than their own.[2] As a result,
they cannot even begin to assess the risks and costs of going global.

It turns out that the globalization of business *processes* has in some ways preceded the globalization of business *knowledge*.

At one U.S. company, for example, the chief legal officer complained that although her CEO and his executive team had made an acquisition of a British company with extensive operations in Brazil, the U.S. firm did so without any real understanding of their legal liabilities in Brazil, especially regarding existing employment contracts and obligations, should they decide to shut down any operations in Brazil. The CEO and his team proceeded as if the rules and customs in Brazil were no different from the rules and customs in Atlanta, where the company was based, or London, where the acquired company was headquartered. The CEO's strategy called for rationalizing operations in Brazil by combining offices and dismissing some people, even though no one on the senior management team understood the liabilities those firings would incur. Furthermore, the CEO, CFO, their lawyers, and the extended U.S. management team did not really understand Brazil's culture of corruption. Finally, although they were bound by the Foreign Corrupt Practices Act, they did not grasp its power and reach. The company found itself exposed on three CLEAR factors—corruption, legal, and regulatory—which significantly impacted its ability to conduct business successfully and profitably. None of these three risk areas were examined during the due diligence process.

In another set of discussions around opacity, which took place in Midland, Michigan, executives at Dow Chemical Company explained to us that they had structured their acquisition of Union Carbide, the chemical company responsible for the 1984 Bhopal industrial accident, in such a way as to make Union Carbide a Dow subsidiary, rather than an integrated business unit within the parent company. In doing so, Dow thought it was protected from any outstanding obligations relating to Union Carbide and its Indian operations. But Dow did not really understand the way Indian politicians think. For decades, Indian politicians have used the Bhopal incident and the rusted remains of the old Union Carbide plant to emphasize the "evils" of foreign investment. As a result, Dow didn't simply acquire a chemical company; it acquired India's national symbol of everything that's wrong with globalization. The Dow executives proved that even a large, sophisticated multinational company can sometimes go about globalizing in a parochial way.

These examples and countless others we shall discuss in this book—including Parmalat, Royal Ahold, Barings Bank, and Daiwa Securities—show that companies usually need support assessing the costs associated with opacity risks when making global decisions. While decentralization increases efficiency and speeds up decision making, it also increases a company's overall risks and potential exposure to the high costs of opacity.

Our research indicates that opacity's costs to business are far-reaching. There is a strong relationship between small-scale, high-frequency business risks and an unhealthy investment environment comprised of slow growth, lackluster foreign direct investment, flagging equity markets, and a host of other woes. Based upon a simple set of regression analyses, we have determined that each one point increase in an Opacity Index score correlates with:

- *A decrease in average per capita income of $986 a year.*
  This slows growth, consumer spending, and the ability of a country to make productive investments. It is also a dramatic reminder that while opacity may benefit a few, it always hurts the many. The struggle up from poverty is greatly slowed by opacity.

- *Lower net foreign direct investment as a percent of GDP by 1 percent.* This retards the transfer of technology and serves as a drag on growth and the globalization of the economy. In emerging markets, foreign direct investment plays the same role as venture capital in developed markets. It transfers technology and kick-starts the economy.

- *Lower Capital Access Index scores by 0.06 points.* This results in less entrepreneurship and fewer new business formations. Access to capital is one of only a handful of paths up from poverty, especially in high population growth countries.

- *Lower bank assets as a percent of GDP by 4 percent.* High opacity is one reason many emerging market countries prefer putting their money in Switzerland, the United Kingdom, or the United States rather than keeping it at home where it can be reinvested.

- *Lower stock market capitalization as a percent of GDP by 0.9 percent.* Countries like India and China and regions like the Middle East have until recently struggled to create viable financial markets due to high levels of opacity. Most big investors prefer well-regulated markets to those that are opaque.

- *Lower stock market traded value as a percent of GDP by 0.9 percent.* Companies traded in high-opacity countries are usually traded at a discount to their value because of opacity risks and the inability of investors to look at the books.

- *Increased average borrowing interest rate by 57 basis points.* Interest rates track with risk. The more opaque a country, the higher the lending rate. High interest rates are not only a drag on growth but tie the hands of policymakers when times get tough.

- *Increased inflation rate by 0.46 percent.* When opacity permeates a society, it adds to the cost of everything.

This chapter reviews the costs of opacity in detail, ending with three case studies that exemplify why businesses should, or rather, why they *must* seriously consider these costs when going global. Businesses that do not pay attention to a country's level of opacity could find that they are making long-term business decisions based on unrealistic estimates of risk and return.

A Caveat: Risks and Costs Vary by Industry

Before diving into the detailed analysis of opacity's costs, it is important to note that, in almost every case, costs are relative to the type of business. This is an important piece of information to which few companies pay sufficient heed. For example, the opacity costs of locating a medical company in France are higher than the opacity costs of locating a raw materials company in France. France, which scores well in areas of enforcement policy, accounting standards, and regulatory oversight, scores poorly when it comes to legal issues. Whereas France is not as legally contentious as the United States, if you do get into trouble in France and need the courts to resolve your dispute, you had better be patient. Slow-to-change industries that do not need brand or patent protection, such as raw materials, can often resolve their conflicts without resorting to the courts. However, a company in a fast-moving business like high-tech or biotech, where patent rights are critical, may rely heavily on the legal system for protection.

As a result, the "L" factor in CLEAR is both an independent and dependent variable. It is independent because getting a case heard or resolved is subject to a number of objective processes. It is dependent because its importance is dictated by the type of company under consideration and the sector in which it is engaged. If a patent infringement process takes a decade to reach a conclusion, it can result in the destruction of a company whose business edge depended on the protection of its intellectual property.

The Costs of Opacity Detailed

Business decisions are hard enough to execute successfully under the complex circumstances of rapidly changing markets. When costs are hidden, the impact on business plans and financial transactions can be devastating. In this section, we examine and quantify the hidden costs of opacity.

Cost to Growth: High Opacity Means Lower per Capita GDP

Real GDP per capita is a common and important measure of a county's economic development. Although businesses typically assess GDP per capita as a stand-alone variable, this statistic is closely tied to a country's opacity. As shown in figure 2-1, a regression

FIGURE 2-1

Opacity score negatively correlated with GDP

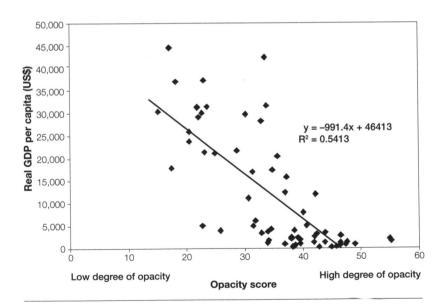

$$y = -991.4x + 46413$$
$$R^2 = 0.5413$$

analysis of real GDP per capita plotted against a country's Opacity Index scores produces a negative and statistically significant relationship. This indicates that countries with low per capita GDPs tend to have higher levels of opacity on average, whereas richer countries have lower levels. Furthermore, each of the CLEAR components is negatively and, in statistical terms, significantly correlated with per capita GDP at the 1-percent level.

Countries with lower than median Opacity Index scores have an average per capita real GDP of $20,500, whereas those with higher than median scores have an average per capita real GDP of only $3,100. This difference in average per capita real GDP is statistically significant at the 1-percent level.

Cost to Investment: Opacity Reduces Net Foreign Direct Investment

Foreign direct investment (FDI) has a positive impact on economic growth and development because it represents the amalgamation of stable investment funds, advanced technology, efficient managerial skills, and easier access to the world market. However, our research suggests that opacity has negative and significant impacts on FDI relative to GDP, as shown in figure 2-2. For every one point increase in the Opacity Index, FDI as a percent of GDP is lowered by 1 percent. Conversely, higher levels of FDI are given to countries with a more transparent financial and economic system.

One might take pause with this finding. What of a country like China, which has high levels of opacity and high levels of economic development? We have found that the simple lure of China's "bigness" has tended to offset its risks. As a result, China is an anomaly, receiving a greater share of investment than would otherwise be warranted. However, the results of this study indicate that if China were to become more transparent, the amount of FDI would likely increase.

FIGURE 2-2

Opacity score and foreign direct investment

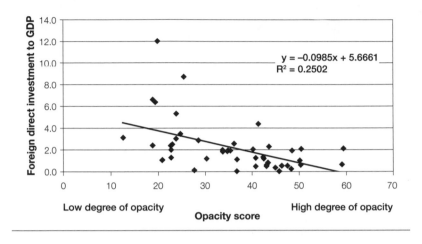

Cost of Capital: Opacity Increases the Capital Costs

The third, and quite important, cost of opacity has to do with its effect on the price of capital. Because risks are higher in high-opacity countries, capital is generally scarcer and higher priced. We assessed opacity's relationship to capital costs using several measures. As suggested by the analysis across these measures, the information asymmetries generated by opacity through corruption, legal, enforcement, accounting, and regulatory means affects the costs of capital. This has a chilling effect upon entrepreneurial growth and innovation, as well as the cost of funds for all projects and enterprises.

Measuring cost of capital using borrowing interest rates. High-opacity countries tend to fall into two groups regarding cost of capital as it pertains to borrowing rates:

1. Countries reliant on foreign investment. In many cases, high-opacity countries with limited domestic availability of

capital suffer from underdevelopment. This is especially true if information is not properly disclosed to investors who are deciding where to place their funds. In these countries, international investors may be reluctant to fund projects if they are uncertain that funds will be allocated to their purported uses. Unless these countries have special attributes—the presence of oil, gas, or certain raw materials—often the only source of capital is from foreign aid, which is also often limited.

2. Countries that may provide investment capital through "non-market" means. In a number of high- and medium-opacity countries—China and Japan, for example—capital is plentiful and cheap because of what John Maynard Keynes calls "financial repression."[3] In these countries, governments penalize savers by enforcing below-market interest rates and by limiting where they can put their money. As a result, capital is available and inexpensive if you are a borrower, but expensive if you are a saver. In places where financial repression is high, pensioners bear a disproportionate share of the costs of growth.

In addition, some large countries are able to borrow internationally in hard currency at low interest rates—in some instances at rates below the premium expected based solely on their opacity score. This apparent anomaly is not an error in calculation. Rather, it results from a combination of market dynamics and government policies: countries that borrow in international capital markets are typically obliged to service their debts in hard currency, such as U.S. dollars. They are accordingly able to borrow at lower interest rates than would otherwise be the case. However, when the same countries float domestic bond issuances, the interest rates are typically much higher. As a result, opacity contributes to the inability of some countries to borrow in their own currencies.

Regardless of the category a high-opacity country falls into, the cost of capital as measured by borrowing rates is undoubtedly affected by opacity-related risks within that country because investors seek a premium, of sorts, to compensate for unreliable or costly information. Not surprisingly, the correlation between opacity and the cost of capital, as measured by borrowing interest rates, proves to be, on average, positive. A regression analysis indicates that countries with low opacity have significantly lower borrowing interest rates than countries with higher opacity.

What do these conclusions mean? Companies operating in low-opacity countries have an edge over those operating in high-opacity countries, all other things being equal. This becomes especially important over the long term. Though companies are racing to do business in the high-opacity BRIC countries—Brazil, Russia, India, and China—they may find themselves better off doing business in the "Edge" countries: Chile, Taiwan, Thailand, Malaysia, Israel, and Korea. Whereas labor costs in these countries are higher and populations are smaller than those in the BRIC countries, the Edge countries have an advantage because they are relatively transparent—though not nearly as transparent as the Index's top-scoring countries.

As a result, risks in these countries are lower than in the BRIC countries and capital is plentiful. Taiwan, Malaysia, Thailand, and Korea may not have as many workers as in China, and Israel may not have as many software engineers as in India, but doing business in these countries is less risky and there are far fewer hidden costs. Surprisingly, this statement holds true even when Israel's war-related risks are taken into account. While dramatic, these risks have been shown to have a very limited effect on that country's economy, markets, and rates of growth.

Measuring cost of capital using loans, bonds, and equity. When we began our work, we asked respondents from the surveyed countries about the typical terms faced by firms (for example, cost, currency of issuance, duration) when raising capital through the three main types of financial instruments: loans, bonds, and equity.

To better understand the relationship between opacity and typical issuance terms, the countries have been divided into two groups. The midpoint of the range of opacity scores—35 points—has been adopted as the cut-off point between "low-opacity" and "high-opacity" countries. This division places 30 countries in the low-opacity score group (15–35) and 10 in the high-opacity score group (35–55).[4]

Figure 2-3 shows the average cost of capital for firms in lower opacity countries by type of financial instrument, as compared to those costs for firms in higher opacity countries. As graphed, the average bank loan rate in lower opacity countries is significantly lower than in high opacity countries. Likewise, investors in less opaque countries demand an average return that is lower than in more opaque countries. These higher rates of interest, due to opacity, act as a drag on growth and slow new business formations.

FIGURE 2-3

Opacity index and cost of capital by financial instruments

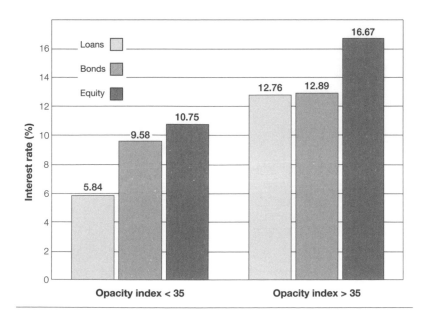

Furthermore, the ability or willingness of firms in more opaque countries to raise capital on a longer-term basis is reduced, in comparison to firms in less opaque countries. Figure 2-4 charts average duration to maturity of loans and bonds, showing that firms in countries with lower opacity obtain loans with longer durations than in countries with higher opacity. The same is true for bonds.

Measuring cost of capital using government bonds and nominal lending rate. We analyzed additional measures, government bond yield and nominal lending rate, to determine how opacity impacts the cost of public and private capital. We analyzed both due to the lack of a universally accepted measure of a country's cost of capital.[5] The government bond yield refers to "one or more series representing yields to maturity of government bonds or other bonds that

FIGURE 2-4

Opacity index and cost of capital by the maturity of loans and bonds

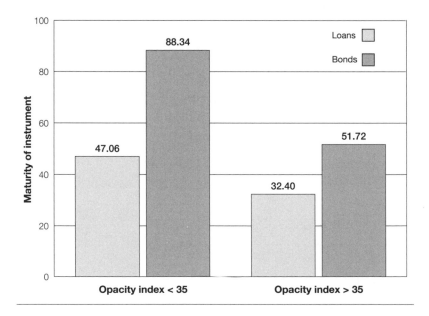

would indicate longer term rates."[6] The nominal lending rate is "the bank rate that usually meets the short- and medium-term financing needs of the private sector." The data series ranges from the first quarter of 2000 to the second quarter of 2001.[7] In both cases, we found a positive and significant correlation between opacity and the cost of capital as measured by each spread.

Measuring cost of capital using the Milken Institute Capital Access Index. Finally, we measured the cost of capital using the Capital Access Index (CAI), a quantitative measure that ranks countries on the basis of entrepreneurs' access to capital.[8] This Index, issued annually by the Milken Institute, is based on a number of variables, including equity market capitalization, market liquidity, interest rate volatility, and risk of expropriation. To the extent that opacity adversely affects the development and efficiency of financial markets, one would expect the Opacity Index and CAI to be significantly correlated. A simple bivariate regression relating the Opacity Index scores to CAI scores, illustrated in figure 2-5, shows that opacity does indeed decrease the size and efficiency of financial markets. Furthermore, each of the CLEAR components is negatively and, in statistical terms, significantly correlated with the CAI at the 1-percent level.

Cost of Lack of Financial Infrastructure: Opacity Retards Development of Financial Systems

We believe a country's financial system is, in many ways, its most important intangible asset. The institutional capacity to generate and pool savings and then invest them in projects and enterprises that will maximize a country's material well-being is critical. To the extent that the size of a country's financial system is closely related to its entrepreneurs' ability to access capital, we would further expect to find a significantly negative correlation between opacity and the

FIGURE 2-5

Opacity score negatively correlated with capital access index

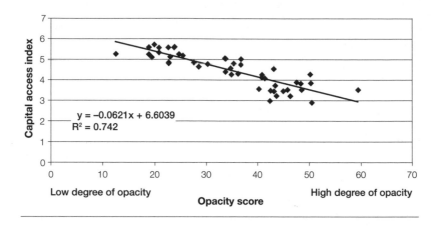

$$y = -0.0621x + 6.6039$$
$$R^2 = 0.742$$

Low degree of opacity — Opacity score — High degree of opacity

degree of development of the financial system.[9] We turned to an analysis of financial sector components to test our hypothesis.

Opacity Index negatively correlated with the size of banking systems. We found that high levels of opacity serve as a brake on the size of the banking system. A regression analysis demonstrated a statistically significant negative relationship between the size of a country's banking system and the Opacity Index: for every point increase in the Opacity Index, bank assets as a percent of GDP drops by four percent. That is, the more opaque a country, the smaller its financial system as measured by bank assets. Additionally, each of the CLEAR components is significantly negative at the 5-percent level. Furthermore, countries that are more transparent than the median of our sample have an average banking sector size equal to 190 percent of GDP, whereas those less transparent than the median have, on average, a banking sector that is just 61 percent of GDP.

We believe this is because opacity increases problems of asymmetric information for banks. Simply put, banks in many countries cannot understand the true creditworthiness of their borrowers; loans are made that would not have otherwise been granted. Conversely, in some situations, banks lend to friends, no matter their credit rating, and to each other. In addition, asymmetric information raises agency costs, and perhaps also raises the likelihood and costs of debtor defaults.

Opacity Index negatively correlated with the size of equity markets. As with the banking sector, we would expect a significant negative relationship between the capitalization of a country's equity markets and its degree of opacity. Research has shown that opacity can lead to wider bid-offer spreads and hence less liquid and less efficient financial markets.[10] Additionally, opacity can mask the underlying fundamentals of investments, thereby making investment in an opaque country less attractive. This in turn generates an opacity-related risk premium for firms in more opaque countries when they raise capital.

We find that the Opacity Index has a statistically significant and negative correlation with stock market capitalization. Again, each of the CLEAR components is also significantly negative at the 5-percent level or less. We are also able to determine that countries more transparent than the median have an average equity market capitalization equal to 106 percent of GDP, whereas those more opaque than the median have an average equity market capitalization of only 30 percent of GDP. This difference in average equity market size is significant at the 1-percent level.

Opacity Index negatively correlated with financial structure. Finally, we analyzed the correlation between opacity and the ratio of stock market capitalization to banking sector size. This analysis shows us if an individual country's financial system—whether it is market-based or bank-based—matters with regard to opacity.

The correlation coefficient (R^2) for the Opacity Index score with equity market size is slightly stronger than for banking sector size. If this difference in correlations is due to a greater sensitivity of market-based financial systems to the lack of transparent practices, then one might expect to find a negative correlation between opacity and the degree to which a country's financial system is market-based. As shown in figure 2-6, we do indeed find a statistically significant negative relationship between the Opacity Index and the ratio of stock market capitalization to bank assets. Additionally, we find that the corruption and regulatory components of CLEAR are negatively related to financial system structure at the 10-percent level of significance. We did not, however, find that the average ratio of equity market capitalization to banking assets for countries less opaque than the median is in statistical terms significantly different from the average ratio for countries more opaque than the median.

The results of this examination of the correlation between opacity and the size of financial systems are intriguing and troubling.

FIGURE 2-6

Opacity score negatively correlated with financial structure

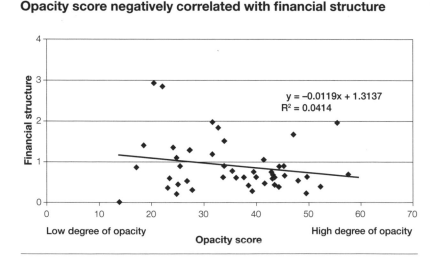

They suggest a role for increased transparency among the factors that stimulate the growth of this important economic sector. Both financial institutions and financial markets are critical to the infrastructure of investment flows within countries and their ability to build a broad-based business community capable of generating wealth and income. Financial services are crucial for firm creation, industrial expansion, and economic growth.

Cost of Tax Equivalents: High Opacity Results in a "Hidden Tax" for Investors

Both taxes and opacity tend to discourage productive investment. This parallel suggests the value of looking at the effect of opacity as if it were a hidden tax. The term "tax equivalent" refers to an increase in the corporate tax rate that reduces inward FDI by the same amount as an increase in opacity from the level prevailing in certain low-opacity, top-scoring countries to the level of opacity for the country in question.[11] In simpler words, how much opacity equals how much tax?

We use a three-step procedure to compute the tax equivalent cost of opacity. First, for any given country not in the benchmark group, we look at how much higher its opacity level is relative to the highest opacity score in the topmost group (that is, an actual opacity score of 30). Second, we use a regression framework to estimate how much a given increase in opacity and corporate tax rate would discourage inward FDI, taking into account the effects on investment of other characteristics of the country. From the regression estimates, we can infer the relationship between a unit of increase in the tax rate and a unit of increase in opacity. Third, by combining the information in the first two steps, we can estimate the tax equivalent for each country's opacity level in excess of the opacity prevailing in the benchmark countries.

For example, the Philippines' opacity score is 50, far below the opacity levels of the United Kingdom, Finland, Hong Kong, United

States, and other top-ranking countries. As a result, the Philippines' inward FDI suffers relative to that of the top-scoring countries. The Philippines' opacity score is the equivalent to an increase in the corporate tax rate of 66 percent.[12] Russia's opacity score is 45—fully 31 points higher than the top-scoring United Kingdom. In terms of its impact on FDI, this level of opacity is similar to raising the corporate tax rate by 41 percent higher than the United Kingdom.

These impressively large numbers illustrate that the cost of opacity is quantitatively important for a number of reasons: First, the term "tax equivalent" equates opacity with tax in terms of discouraged investment. However, tax and opacity are not equivalent in one important respect: while tax can potentially generate revenue for the government to provide public services, opacity has the opposite effect. It generates no revenue for the government and produces no additional services, which presumably taxes are supposed to do.

Second, the tax-equivalent effect of opacity is based on estimates of the effects of tax and opacity on foreign direct investment. This focus on foreign investment is chosen for several reasons: (1) bilateral foreign investment offers a richer and larger data set than domestic investment numbers; (2) international investment data is more comparable across countries than domestic investment data, and cross-country comparison is one of the objectives of this report; (3) most countries in the world are now eager to attract foreign direct investment because they recognize the positive contribution of foreign investment to their domestic economic growth. We may further note that the tax equivalent effect of opacity in terms of discouraging *domestic* investment is likely to be similar.

Finally, many governments in the world now offer generous tax giveaways to attract foreign investment. Our findings on tax equivalency suggest that if these governments can succeed in reducing the level of opacity across many or all of the CLEAR dimensions, the impact on foreign investment is likely to be much like that of a tax concession, without the attendant loss of revenue to the government. Furthermore, for business, the effect of lowering opacity is equivalent to decreasing overall costs.

Case Studies: How Much Does Opacity Cost Specific Countries?

Opacity scores are relative measures of the attractiveness of one country over another. In a world where capital is highly mobile and countries compete for it, opacity scores are useful decision-making tools for portfolio and direct investors. The case studies that follow offer comparisons between countries to show in more detail how opacity scores work.

Finland Versus Russia

One only has to consider the difference between Finland (score of 17) and Russia (score of 45) to see the costs of opacity at work. Both countries, especially during the Cold War, were poor, even though they had both invested heavily in education. Both countries were rich in minerals, although only Russia had oil. When the Cold War ended, Russia and Finland each took a different course.

Russian capitalism developed with very high levels of opacity—especially regarding corruption and lack of legal protections. Russia also had a poorly functioning regulatory structure for its businesses, few real legal protections, and a vague set of laws governing such things as property rights. As a result, Russia, despite its oil wealth, declined economically for more than a decade despite the end of the Cold War.

Finland, on the other hand, started on a path to development that emphasized low levels of opacity through the creation of strong institutions, regulatory structures, and laws. According to our research, corruption in Finland is almost nonexistent.

What was the result of Finland's low-opacity development strategy? Finland now has one of the most vibrant economies in the world and was ranked at the top of the World Economic Forum's competitiveness index of eighty countries for 2003–2004.[13] Russia, by contrast, lies at the bottom of the Index. "During the cold war, Finland had no presence at all in the telecommunications sector. It did not even have 'also-ran' status. It simply wasn't a contender," said Ed Sim, a partner at DawnTrader, a global venture capital fund in New York, which invests in the telecommunications sector. "Today, Finland is one of a handful of countries that leads the world in that sector," Sim said.

Mexico Versus China

Businesses need to understand how much *extra* a high-opacity country costs over a low-opacity country. Mexico, for example, which has an opacity score of 43, requires a return of 5.01 percent above the U.S. rate of return in order to offset its risk. China, by contrast, with a score of 48, requires a premium on the U.S. rate of return of 6.49 percent to offset its risk. What this means to managers is that in some instances, China, with its low wage rates, may be actually be a less attractive place to do business than Mexico when the risks are factored in. A look at the individual CLEAR factors can provide managers with even more understanding when making their decisions since not all companies are sensitive in the same way to each type of small-scale, high-frequency risk.

Jamaica Versus Singapore

At the end of World War II, high-opacity Jamaica and low-opacity Singapore (score of 28) had nearly identical GDPs and the same level of per capita income.[14] However, Singapore is a highly developed, rich country today while Jamaica remains poor. This is despite the fact that both countries are island nations and that Jamaica has the benefit of being much closer to its largest market, the United States. In addition, Jamaica has raw materials (bauxite) while Singapore has none.

In their post–World War II histories, the countries suffered similar low-frequency, high-impact problems related to weather. But where these two countries really differed was that Singapore set out to eradicate its high-frequency, low-impact problems whereas Jamaica did nothing about them. Money allocated toward investment—whether in education or new factories—was put to its intended use in Singapore, whereas it was put into someone's pocket in Jamaica.

The ultimate cost of opacity is lack of growth. This can be seen in the difference between Jamaica, with a per capita GDP of $3,928 in 2006, and Singapore, with a per capita GDP of $28,939.[15] This astounding difference is accounted for by programs planned, but never fully funded, in Jamaica, due to theft and inefficiency in how the country is run.

Costs in the Open

The costs of opacity are many and significant. For business, there are obvious implications. Managers need to make decisions based on more than the size of a country's market and the price of its labor. They need to take into account how its economy works beyond these factors. By understanding opacity, managers can take precautions. If they have a choice of where to locate a regional headquarters, for example, they might choose a country that scores higher on legal and economic factors. If they are looking for a place to build a plant, they may care more about corruption measures. If they are looking at joint-venturing with another company, they may focus on legal measures to help them think about how the provisions of a joint-venture contract will be enforced.

This is not to suggest that businesses avoid high-opacity countries. Indeed, in some areas of commerce such as mineral extraction and oil production, avoiding countries would prove difficult, since many of the largest producers of raw materials and oil have high opacity scores. Instead, business should use the Index to prudently measure risks and to create mechanisms to protect against such costs.

It is in everyone's interest for companies and countries to work together to bring down a country's opacity scores. For businesses, it is critical in order to become fully global in a prudent way. For countries, it is necessary in order to grow, develop, and attract their fair share of inbound investment.

Chapter Three

Corruption

O N DECEMBER 2, 1984, a Union Carbide plant in Bhopal, India exploded, spewing twenty-seven tons of deadly methyl isocyanate gas into the air. As many as half a million people were exposed to the gas and twenty thousand died either immediately or in the ensuing years. Many survivors were blinded and had terrible lung damage. It was the deadliest industrial accident in history.

Rashmi Mayur, a Yale-educated Indian environmentalist, was involved in the negotiations between Union Carbide (now part of Dow Chemical) and the Indian government. Shortly after the explosion, Rashmi visited with Warren Anderson, then chairman of Union Carbide. He also visited with Ed Meese, the U.S. Attorney General at the time, and with many Indian and American corporate and government officials. On the table was a monetary settlement between India and the U.S. chemical company to compensate the victims' families and care for injured survivors. The fund was also supposed to pay for removing remaining toxins from the area, tearing down the destroyed plant, and building a hospital.

As Rashmi reported to one of us, during the negotiations he was offered a 1 percent "facilitation fee" to bring the negotiations to a speedy end at a favorable price. He was vague about which parties had offered him the fee. Since the initial settlement numbers discussed were as high at $3 billion, his facilitation fee could have been substantial. But Rashmi was an honorable man. He refused the offer, but kept the information to himself; he stated that, given the level of the people offering the payment, he could have gotten into more trouble had he reported it to the authorities.

Despite a final settlement (Union Carbide agreed to pay $470 million in 1989), the area around Bhopal has not been fully cleansed of toxins and the old plant has not been torn down. And while the Indian government claims that half a million people received compensation, many in India dispute whether the Indian government released the settlement money into the right hands.

Whether and to whom facilitation payments were made is anybody's guess. We have no evidence, other than Rashmi's statement, that people were offered bribes to facilitate an agreement. Even so, India scores very high on the Opacity Index, especially in the area of corruption.

Corruption Issues Defined

As defined by Transparency International, a global organization fighting corruption, corruption is "the abuse of entrusted power for private gain."[1] Corruption was often considered culturally bound or explained away as being the necessary grease to lubricate the wheels of government and the economy. Yet increasingly, these rationalizations have faltered as the destructive effects of corruption have increased.

There are two main elements to corruption, argues Tim Hartford in a March 2006 series of articles on Cameroon and other corrupt countries in the *Financial Times*: first, a leader who expects to remain in power for several years and who only helps his economy in order to profit personally; second, bureaucrats who wish to profit personally by charging additional fees to do what they are supposed to do. Fees charged by bureaucrats are typically not cheap. Hartford describes how a small business in Cameroon is required to spend nearly as much as the average Cameroonian makes in two years on official and unofficial fees. In real estate transactions, hidden and governmental fees typically end up costing about a fifth of the property's value. To get the courts to enforce an unpaid invoice takes nearly two years, costs more than a third of the invoice's value, and requires fifty-eight separate procedures. No wonder Cameroon, a country of great beauty, valuable raw materials, rich agriculture, and tremendous potential for creating wealth, just manages to scrape by. Poverty is rampant, with political leaders and bureaucrats stifling the country's ability to create wealth.

The experience of corruption can be unnerving. What one might think is a substantive meeting with a governmental official to renegotiate external debt or negotiate a supply contract can turn quietly into something entirely different. Instead of exchanging official business cards at the conclusion of the meeting, one might receive the private business card of the official's local corporate connection—a local bank or mining company, perhaps—with a mention that an "associate" will follow up. When the discrete follow-up call comes, a side conversation central to the main project ensues, as cash or other requirements are discussed as means to move the project forward. Without the so-called "side deal," there is no deal at all.

In several instances of which we are aware, governmental officials been sufficiently brazen, and the atmosphere so permissive, that payments—that is, payoffs—have been specified in writing. In one example of this type of behavior, a South Korean government official asked one of us for a personal payment of $25,000 to expedite an already approved $250,000 research contract! Without that payment, the note explained, the approved amount could fall victim to government red tape.

Foreign investment and business activities are disrupted daily by corruption. No country, company, or institution is immune. Courts around the world are clogged with cases wherein construction companies have been accused of paying bribes to local officials to win World Bank projects. Pharmaceutical companies are in the courts in Asia, in particular, fighting against corrupt officials who turn a blind eye to drug counterfeiting. American defense contractors have been accused of hiring Pentagon officials on special "consulting" contracts to facilitate the sale of airplanes and arms to the Department of Defense.

At a diplomatic gathering at the United Nations, which one of us attended, a Costa Rican government official whispered to one of us that he could issue passports from his country to people in need of them for a fee of $50,000.

In the last decade or two, officials at the highest levels in Japan, Sweden, Canada, Germany, France, Britain, the United States, and many other "advanced, developed" countries have been caught peddling their countries' wares and lining their pockets at the same time. Not only is this type of behavior illegal, but when prime ministers, presidents, and defense officials are accused of corrupt behavior, it throws in doubt their motives across the board.

Direct Costs of Corruption

While participants in corruption schemes may believe their actions are benefiting them, their corporations, or their projects, they seldom identify the direct costs related to their behavior, namely, time, resources, and money. Corruption can appear in a number of guises. Klaus Uhlenbruck and Jonathan Doh at the Mays Business School at Texas A&M have identified these arenas and surveyed the various costs they impose:

- Bribe-seeking

- Additional red tape

- Disinvestment by established companies

- Imposition of unproductive costs

- Undermining of legal institutions

- Engagement with organized crime and gangs[2]

Bribes

Slick notes, grease, baksheesh, mordida, kickbacks, bribes—all of these terms are associated with the most obvious form of corruption. Improper payments to push sales, ensure discounts, or grant favors create direct costs for business. ITT, Lockheed Martin, Xerox, Procter & Gamble, and many other corporations have periodically been caught up in scandals that did tremendous monetary and reputation damage to these firms, compromising their competitive position to do business in various countries.

Bribes result in increased start-up and operational costs. Moreover, the secrecy of bribes creates additional uncertainty that the official receiving the bribe will perform as promised, thereby further diminishing the incentive to invest. A business cartoon in Canada recently reflected this dynamic, showing a group of businessmen around a conference table and the CEO stating: "Relax, we have nothing to hide that hasn't already been hidden."

Bureaucratic Delays and Red Tape

In negotiating through the typical red tape and bureaucratic delays associated with doing business, especially in a foreign country, a company may face time delays which yield increased costs. However, certain governments or businesses may impose additional red tape as a means to encourage illegal payments to "speed up the process." These formally legal procedures create opportunities for corruption as businesses seek to overcome time-consuming barriers through informal, personal payments to business or government officials.

Disinvestment

In attempting to avoid the rent-seeking behavior of corrupt officials or business partners, business operators may be forced to shirk
transparency in their business dealings and limit investment exposure. Hiding output and profits increases the cost of operations and
opens businesses to other risks. Additionally, these costs and risks
inevitably burden legitimate business activity. Ultimately, the result
could be that businesses may opt out of a country entirely to forgo
losses due to the high costs of corruption.

Unproductive Costs

A range of unproductive costs not related to a company's operations may be forced upon a business due to corruption. Lobbying, vote
solicitation, donations to "charities," employing relatives of local business or government officials, or other unrelated transactions, often
under the rubric of "profit sharing" with government officials, encum-
ber a basic business proposition and the projections of profitability. In
Thailand, for example, gifts to public officials are a common part of
patron-client relationships. Perhaps the greatest linguistic example of
corruption's penetration is from Papua New Guinea. In that country,
the "wantok system" (literally, "one talk" or "those who speak a common language") is based upon officials appointing friends and relatives
to highly paid positions, thereby enabling loyalty, as opposed to skill
and performance, as a determinant of political and economic power.[3]
As with bribes, the result of these costs may damage more than a company's bottom line, as these costs may impact a business's reputation.

Compromising Legal Institutions and Engaging Organized Crime

By its very nature, corruption undermines legal and enforcement institutions. When faced with a corrupt proposal, as Rashmi

Mayur was in the Union Carbide story, businesses may hesitate to rely on traditional means of resolution, as doing so may result in greater penalties. As businesses turn away from existing legal and enforcement structures, the costs (and risks) of enforcing contracts increase. In some cases, the legal system itself may be corrupt, yielding even higher costs. Businesses may have to rely upon other, less desirable forms of security. For example, the post-Soviet republics have become heralded for their market for "protection" and "security." The informality and criminal nature of these markets undermines the provision of these services. That is because the aims of the people providing security and protection are mercenary rather than altruistic and because they operate outside of strict legal controls. If someone were to offer a night watchman a higher fee than a building or business owner, he might turn his head (or offer his keys) to a gang of thugs seeking entrance into a building. One of us has seen forms of this behavior operate in Nairobi, Kenya, where a common complaint among urban dwellers is that their apartments are often robbed by the watchmen they employ to protect them and their property.

Indirect Costs of Corruption

In addition to direct costs, corruption has profound indirect costs. Most notably, an increasing wave of research shows a relationship between higher levels of corruption and slower long-term growth.[4] Overall, the indirect costs of corruption include:

- Retarding economic growth

- Misallocating human capital

- Distorting government expenditure

- Reducing the efficacy of aid

- Increasing occurrence and severity of currency and banking crises

- Greater market volatility

- Lower shareholder value in local stock markets

- More restrictions of capital accounts, increasing financial rigidity, and the likelihood of monetary crises

Retarding Economic Growth

When public power is abused for private benefit, prices are artificially inflated beyond their cost of production and distribution. Economists are rife with terms for this: market failure, perverse incentives, distorted production functions, to name a few. Countries vary widely in their institutional framework to inhibit corruption-induced market distortions. Business decision making is difficult enough with just weighing the risks and uncertainties of markets. The added weight and opacity of corruption further complicates and inhibits business and investment decisions.

International direct and portfolio investment is vital to developing countries. By disrupting it, corruption becomes a source of international macroeconomic instability due to the level and composition of capital flows. Research conducted by Shang-Jin Wei at the Brookings Institution has shown that an increase in a country's corruption level from low—such as that in Singapore—to high, such as that in Indonesia, has the same negative effect on inward foreign direct investment as raising the corporate tax rate by 50 percent.[5] Moreover, he shows that the most dependable kind of foreign investors—those disposed to long-term commitments to projects and businesses—often refuse to put their money into countries where corrupt officials prey upon the private sector. Because the International Monetary Fund and governments have provided more insurance to lenders than to director investors, investment funds become skewed toward short-term loans. There is a growing body of research on the impact of corruption in investment, GDP growth, institutional quality, government expenditure, poverty, shareholder value, international flows of capital, composition of capital, goods, and aid.

Misallocating Human Capital

Human capital is also misallocated as a result of corruption. Financial incentives lure talented and educated individuals into corruption schemes, and away from productive activity. The accumulation of political capital replaces financial capital accumulation as the outcome of corrupt systems. With political capital stored up by a select few, favors are granted (such as special operating licenses and no-bid contracts) that lead to profits. And, when entire societies operate under these conditions people begin to view many non-productive forms of behavior as the norm.

Distorting Government Expenditure

Government expenditure is distorted by corruption since government officials are enticed to respond more to opportunities to extort payments than to chances for improving social welfare. Research shows that more corrupt systems skew investment toward larger infrastructure projects and defense than to social welfare and education.

Reducing Efficacy of Aid

Multilateral organizations involved in foreign aid and investment have been equally vulnerable to corruption. Examples abound in the controversy over Iraq. The investigation of the UN's Oil-for-Food Programme headed by former Federal Reserve Chairman Paul

Volcker yielded many finds.[6] Among them was the case of the Australian Wheat Board (AWB), which paid illegal kickbacks to Saddam Hussein's regime to secure contracts under the Oil-for-Food Programme. According to Volcker's report, between 1999 and 2003, the AWB paid over $221 million to Alia, a Jordanian company, which then made illegal payments to the Iraqi government.[7]

Increasing Financial and Banking Crises

More than half of the member countries of the International Monetary Fund (IMF) have experienced either banking crises or significant financial problems over the past twenty years.[8] Some countries, in fact, have experienced more than one disruptive episode during this relatively short time period. Furthermore, the crises have occurred in countries at all levels of development and in all parts of the world.

The occurrence of banking crises or significant financial problems merits special attention because they can lead to severe disruptions in both a country's payment mechanism and its credit system. Indeed, the estimated costs of such crises have been enormous in many instances, ranging as high as 41 percent of GDP in Chile and 55 percent in Argentina in the early 1980s to 60 percent in South Korea and 80 percent in Indonesia in the late 1990s.[9] The fact that banking and financial crises can be so costly poses difficult challenges and choices and creates potential for cross-border, contagion effects. In Indonesia, where members of parliament were implicated in the collapse of one of its largest banks, the ability to deal with the problem was compromised by a legislature that contributed to the problem.

Greater Market Volatility

Corrupt or "crony" capitalism in Indonesia, Korea, Philippines and Thailand shifted the composition of capital flows toward short-term financing, which made those countries more vulnerable to crises. Corruption acts to repel more stable forms of foreign investment and leaves countries dependent on volatile foreign loans to finance growth. Corruption creates incentives to evade taxes, reducing tax revenues and increasing expenditures, which leads to adverse budgetary consequences. Politically based lending—where loan recipients are those favored by the government—also ended in tears as the Asian, Russian, and Latin American debt crises of recent years attest. Corruption has also been shown to increase macroeconomic volatility, resulting in lower long-term growth rates.

The international financial crisis of the late 1990s demonstrated how corruption, cronyism, and enmeshed political relations in the economic sphere devastated political stability, economic prosperity, and growth. This was true in issues of bribery of public officials as well as in the corruption of police forces, public procurement, and tax administration. The impact of these factors led to suppression of local stock markets and their emergence as a means of investment flows, greater financial system rigidity, and increasing likelihood of and difficulties in resolving monetary and banking crises.[10]

Measuring Corruption: Opacity Index Results

Economists study the impact of corruption on growth, distribution, government expenditures, and foreign direct and portfolio investment. In all cases, these economic impacts also affect the quality of public service delivery, public policies and administration, morale, rule of law, and even life expectancy. Measuring and monitoring this facet of opacity are key for effective reform. From measurement comes an array of recommendations that could strengthen institutions and check government and private concentrations of power. The reduction of corruption can only derive from increased competition, monitoring, reduction in the size of government, and better audit and record-keeping systems.

As illustrated in figure 3-1, the corruption dimension of the Opacity Index explores the regulatory environment of international capital markets in forty-eight countries to determine the risks—whether real or perceived—associated with a country's regulatory structures. It looks at the regulatory structure in this way because not all problems indicate criminal or corrupt behavior. Some regulatory problems—like inadequate financial reporting—can be violated simply through sloppiness and without criminal intent. But even if these requirements are violated by accident, they still have repercussions since investors will be making business decisions based on faulty information.

Detailed statistical surveys and studies are the best at unearthing the pervasive and arbitrary nature of corruption in specific countries. As such, we have used data from other indexes including data from Transparency International to create our assessment of corruption.[11]

The corruption dimension of the Opacity Index examines:

- Costs of corruption originating with business officials

- The extent to which corruption within the political system distorts economic and financial transactions

- The likelihood of demand or acceptance of bribes in the banking and finance sector

- The reported business costs of corruption by country

Our research indicators of corruption tap the pervasiveness of corruption and its arbitrariness. The pervasiveness of corruption is measured by the frequency of requirements for illicit activity. High frequency, with its attendant predictability, might have its advantages in business planning. But corruption can also be arbitrary. Firms may be uncertain about whom to pay for what and when, and whether economic activity can proceed even with payments. Some researchers have utilized survey data on firms to track how arbitrary

FIGURE 3-1

Corruption index 2005

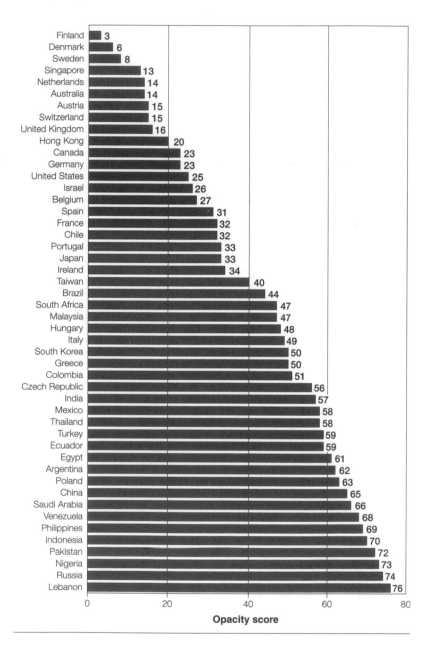

Opacity score

or pervasive corruption is by country, which complements our overall opacity score in categorizing risks. Countries with highly pervasive, but less arbitrary corruption are Argentina, China, Mexico, Nigeria, and Venezuela. Less pervasive, but more arbitrary, corruption exists in Hungary, Malaysia, Poland, and the Czech Republic. Corruption is both pervasive *and* arbitrary in Russia, Egypt, Indonesia, Pakistan, and India. And finally, less pervasive and less arbitrary corruption traditions exist in Italy, South Korea, South Africa, Brazil, and Chile.

How corruption permeates other attributes of economic activity and creates the environment for further opacity will be examined in the chapters that follow.

Case Studies: Examples of Corruption

The *Foreign Corrupt Practices Act of 1977* was enacted principally to prevent corporate bribery of foreign officials. While the act required the keeping of accurate books, records, and accounts by corporations and prohibited bribery by American businesses of foreign officials, it did not address the complexities of business corruption and how it operates.

Institutional Corruption in Japan

Contrary to public belief, problems of corruption don't reside solely in the developing world. Japan provides an interesting case of the institutionalization of corruption within well-guarded bureaucratic operations. In January 2001, Katsutoshi Matsuo, formerly the head of the Japanese Foreign Ministry's Overseas Visit Support Division, was arrested. His job had been to organize trips by prime ministers, diplomats, and other high-ranking governmental officials. Through that process, he managed to deposit Foreign Ministry funds into his personal bank accounts, from which he then paid for trips and trysts, purchased eight golf club memberships, fifteen race-horses, and a luxury Tokyo condominium.[12] In short, Mr. Matsuo was living far beyond a Japanese civil servant's means. Similar scandals were revealed in the Police Department and Ministry of Finance, whereby illicit accounting enabled officials to create slush funds that enabled them to squeeze cash through unofficial channels for unrestricted spending.

In all of the cases reported, the opaqueness of decision making within Japan's bureaucracy created a recipe for taxpayer robbery. In 2001, Japan passed a Freedom of Information Act, but the mere passage of enabling laws does not preclude circumvention. Such transparency laws are only as strong as their enforcers. Lack of disclosure is common in Japan, where responses to allegations of misconduct are often defined by the attempt to "kill complaints with silence." As David Johnson has shown in his studies of bureaucratic corruption in Japan, the corruption has been embedded within the government's powerful Board of Audit, which oversees all ministries, markets, and police, resulting in widespread misuse or toleration of misuse of taxpayers' money.[13] The embedded nature of the corruption has also precluded open reporting of the problem and has torpedoed independent investigations. He found that, due to corruption, only 9 percent of Japanese adults had confidence in the Diet (the Japanese parliament) and only 8 percent had confidence in their national bureaucracy. The comparable confidence figures in the United States, where government is hardly venerated, are 63 percent (for Congress) and 51 percent for the government bureaucracy. The impacts of corruption undermine the basic notion of public voice in democracy. For example, related to this dynamic of corruption's insidious impact upon public confidence, 75 percent of U.S. voters report that their opinions are heard in the nation's policy, while in Japan, only a scant 10 percent feel likewise.[14]

Volkswagen's Trouble with Bribes

According to German law, labor representatives must sit on a company's Board of Directors to advise the business on issues that may impact labor. Such participation is a significant part of the firm's corporate governance.

In the case of German carmaker Volkswagen AG (VW), Klaus Volkert, head of the company's employee council (also known as the "works council"), sat on the VW Board to consult on issues such as the location of new production plants and shortened employee work weeks.[15] In 2005, Volkert and others, including VW's Personnel Chief, Peter Hartz, were charged with forty-four counts of breach of trust for allegedly receiving and providing "special bonuses." Some of the bribes were paid, allegedly, to secure foreign contracts for VW. An audit conducted by KPMG reports that the scandal began with plans to establish a VW plant and dealer network in Angola, Africa. It continued with payments from the government of a southern Indian nation that was also vying for a VW assembly plant.[16] Other bribes were paid to ensure close ties to VW's employee council in exchange for the council's support of key executive issues. With the employee council's approval, VW executives could guarantee support for issues that employees may otherwise disapprove. In January 2007, Hartz was fined $750,000 for paying off labor leaders after acknowledging that he had authorized payments to members of the employee council.

Enabling Corruption in China

Gong Ting, a professor of political science at Syracuse University, conducted a systematic review of corruption problems in China.[17] She found systematic evidence of the institutionalization of collusion across various agencies, enabling embezzlement, state enterprise asset stripping, and other methods of institutional corruption. The study gave us insight into this type of widespread organized corruption scheme, involving smuggling and the complicity of official authorities.

In Zhanjiang in Guangdon Province, approximately one hundred officials were involved in smuggling more than $7.3 billion of goods in return for bribes.[18] The range of government involvement included:

- The customs office

- The antismuggling investigation office, which arranged auctions of smuggled goods

- The city's party chief, who arranged a city loan to finance the smuggling enterprise

- The Vice Mayor

- The port authorities

- The State Tax Bureau

To its credit, China has admitted breaches in ethics and has taken cases of corruption seriously, prescribing severe judgments, including the death penalty and long prison terms. In June 2006, China's National Audit Office said that $1.5 billion in taxes was lost or misappropriated due to corruption. In 2001, the mayor of Xiamen was caught running a $6 billion smuggling ring. China's Communist Party has even gone so far as to declare corruption a "crisis" that could jeopardize the country's growth and stability.

China's "mea culpa" is important. Foreign and portfolio investments have increased dramatically over the past decades and, with them, a persistent exposure to the risks and hidden costs associated with doing business internationally. Because corruption is often hidden from the public and not punished by the courts, it results in transaction costs that are larger than those derived from legal exchanges.[19]

Corruption Costs of Investment in Bulgaria

For many investors, the attraction of low-wage environments and booming market opportunities appears to compensate for the shortcomings of a country's administrative and judicial system in confronting corruption. Bulgaria, however, provides a case where that assumption has been challenged. Investment flows in the country have increased substantially in recent years due to several advantages: privatization sales, accession to the European Union, and relatively skilled labor. Nevertheless, corruption has yielded unanticipated direct and indirect costs to these investments: delays in completing deals, demands for political payments, political interference, and legal challenges by losing bidders in privatizations. Take the case of Advent International, a United States–based private equity group. Advent was selected as the preferred bidder to buy a majority stake in BTC, Bulgaria's public telecommunications operator. But Advent experienced costly delays in completing this deal: it went through thirteen rounds of court hearings over an eighteen-month period before contracts were signed.[20]

Delays this long are especially costly because private equity often uses borrowed money. As a result, the longer it takes to resolve a dispute, the more costly for the borrower.

Nigeria's Anticorruption Campaign

Nigeria has long been legendary for its corruption, but recently hopes have been raised due to its explicit anticorruption campaign. However, critics noted that the campaign was being waged inconsistently. On the one hand, the government was making a concerted effort to eradicate corrupt officials. In March 2005, President Olusegun Obasanjo fired his education minister, Fabian Osuji, after receiving reports that he had inflated his ministry's budget.[21] This came after the labor minister was fired for similar offenses in 2003. On the other hand, corruption continued to run rampant. When Mujahid Dokubo-Asari, a warlord from the oil-rich Niger delta, threatened to wage "all out war" on the Nigerian state if his ethnic kin were not given a bigger share of the oil money, President Obasanjo conceded.[22] As such, confidence in the corruption campaign's application to the critical oil industry remains in doubt.

Corruption in the United States and the United Kingdom

As we have noted, corruption is not specific to emerging markets in foreign lands. The United States and the United Kingdom experience their fair share, especially when government funds play a role in policy decisions.

United States. According to a new paper by Peter Leeson and Russell Sobel of West Virginia University, natural disasters not only destroy properties and disrupt lives, but also encourage corruption.[23] Disaster relief floods money and resources into the affected area, providing public officials the incentive and opportunity to gain wealth through corrupt practices. Their recent research shows that states that receive more disaster relief also have more instances of public corruption. They found that, in the average state, each additional $1 per capita in annual relief received from the Federal Emergency Management Agency (FEMA) increases corruption nearly 2.5 percent.

Their data shows that from 1990 to 2002 more than ten thousand public officials in the United States were convicted of corruption-related crimes. The average was 4 percent nationally, but in Mississippi, Florida, and South Dakota the average was 7.5 percent. Utah, Arizona, and Nebraska, however, have less than half the national average.

United Kingdom. A recent case in the United Kingdom took great pains to argue that bribes are occasionally justified. The interests of national security validated the government's decision to overrule an inquiry into corruption. Britain's Serious Fraud Office (SFO) announced on December 14, 2006 that it would drop its two-year inquiry into bribes that may or may not have been paid by BAE Systems, a defense firm, in exchange for an agreement to supply, organize, and train the Saudi Air Force. In the official announcement, Tony Blair, Britain's prime minister, spoke of the "thousands" of jobs that hung on the contracts, as well as of "ill feeling between us and a key partner and ally" in the fight against Al Qaeda.

Clearly, there is a paradox with Britain's anticorruption efforts. While many thought that this case demonstrated that Britain was adept at keeping dodgy business under wraps, the OECD found it "surprising that no company or individual has been indicted or tried for the offence of bribing foreign public officials."[24]

Dealing Strategically with Corruption

Corruption is endemic, but so what? China may be corrupt, but its vast size still makes it an attractive place to do business. Other countries, such as India, present a similar situation. As a result, companies need to think about corruption strategically. Many claim to do so. Business executives meet to set their globalization strategy. Upon setting what they deem a reasonable business plan, they announce, "we're going to China" (or India or Brazil or the Seychelles). Then they look for an acquisition or for a site upon which to build an outpost or an office. They send a team to the country, telling their lawyers to make certain nothing goes wrong.

But "making certain nothing goes wrong" is often limited to linking up with a local business agent or lawyer and letting the local party handle all the dirty details. In the Middle East, China, and Africa, business agents often do the unmentionable and charge high fees for reaching into their pockets and holding their noses at the same time.

In Mexico, lawyers do that job. In India, Japan, and the Middle East there are business facilitators or "go betweens," as they're called in Japan. Is this any way to run a business?

It isn't, and businesses that rely on this strategy are missing a key challenge: when seeking to go global, they must evaluate all five CLEAR factors, not just one or two. In the business scenarios described above, a relationship with a local partner requires executing a contract that can be enforced so that corruption can be avoided (or, at the very least, minimized). This means that the country's legal system must have a score that is sufficiently low, indicating that legal disputes ("L") can be settled between partners if things go awry. Furthermore, the enforcement ("E") score must be low enough so that there's a cost to breaching a contract.

That doesn't mean all factors must be equal, nor does it mean they all need to be low. It means they must be low enough to protect a company's interests. To avoid corruption in China, for example, the best way to enter business is through a relationship with a Hong Kong company, because Hong Kong companies operate more transparently than Chinese companies do. At other times, the best way into China is through Singapore, also very transparent and very protective of intellectual property.

In any case, the way to operate inside a country requires a strategic assessment of all risks, and not just the risks at hand. Jail or a large fine is a terrible price to pay for abiding by another country's conventions. That means the legal teams back home must understand the global stage. This is rare. It also means that lawyers must become part of a company's strategic discussion—rarer still. With that in mind, we turn to a discussion of the legal dimension of opacity.

Chapter Four

Legal and Enforcement Opacity

W E BEGAN MEASURING opacity in 1999, two years before Enron's troubles were brought to light in 2001. Enron was followed in short order by problems at WorldCom, which—among other things—fabricated billions of dollars in revenues and lent its CEO $400 million to cover his margin calls. Then there was Tyco, where an extravagant CEO and CFO used shareholder money to live life large.[1]

Because these scandals were clustered around the events of September 11, determining how much each of them contributed to the downward economic climate is difficult. In the wake of 9/11 and these corporate disasters, the stock market plunged significantly— from a high of just under 12,000 in 2000 to a low of 7,800 in 2003— which made equity capital far more expensive for companies to acquire, just as our model predicted.

But the American markets recovered. By mid-2006, capital became affordable once again. As a result, mergers and acquisitions increased, as did initial public offerings.

The price of capital in the United States fell markedly as investors regained their faith in the country's ability to police its markets. Indictments were handed down, new legislation—the *Sarbanes-Oxley Act of 2002*—was passed, and enforcement and regulatory agencies were allowed to bare their teeth.[2] Rather than skirt the issue and let the leaders of the scandal-plagued companies off the hook—which might have happened in some countries—America took at least some of them to court. In the end, they were all found guilty and some were sent to jail.[3]

Knowing that investors have recourse is one factor that keeps capital cheap in the United States, Britain, and elsewhere. Investors don't go to markets that are easy; they go to markets where the laws are strict, enforcement is tough, and the guilty are punished. This is a primary reason American markets are as large as they are.

Why Review Legal and Enforcement Opacity Together?

Many emerging market countries are reforming their laws and regulations to make themselves attractive in the eyes of major international investment companies. But it is not only laws that matter. Enforcement of laws and regulations is an integral part of a well-functioning society. Inefficient enforceability of contract laws and property rights force businesses to look for other means of resolving disputes. Efficient law and enforcement structures are necessary complementary structures for managing expectations of investors. In a transparent environment, if a party breaches a contract, the other party can have some expectation of how enforcement of the contract can play out. This expectation is necessary for efficient and effective business engagement. Inability to enforce a contract means fewer business transactions. Thus, value and validity of a contract (including stock, bond, or simple rental agreement) depends on the opaqueness of enforcement and the laws that govern them.

Furthermore, the patterns of variation in enforcement derive from how legal procedures are formalized. Most scholars note that variations in patterns of enforcement derive from the origins of a country's legal system: civil versus common law. These two legal systems are rooted in Roman and English law. They were transplanted through conquest and colonization by France, Germany, and Spain (in the case of civil law) and England (in the case of common law.)

Both domestically evolved and transplanted systems of adjudication face challenges from legal and enforcement opacity. Even systems that are highly formalistic suffer from the problems of more informal systems if the rigidities of legal and enforcement operations bring extreme costs and delays, unwillingness to use the courts, and arbitrary justice. The efficiency of dispute resolution varies widely between countries and regions. Business and economic analysis cannot presume that property and contracts are secured by the courts. Understanding these two factors of opacity together, then, is the best defense in negotiating and analyzing investment and business decisions in the face of legal and enforcement risks and uncertainty.

This chapter will first explore the costs of legal opacity, followed by an exploration of enforcement opacity. It ends with case studies in which both legal and enforcement opacity play a role in the obstruction of successful business operations.

Understanding Legal Systems

It was in Kirkcaldy, Scotland in the early eighteenth century that Adam Smith first observed how moral norms are necessary for an economy to work. For exchange to proceed, contracts must be enforceable, people must have access to information about products and services, and the rule of law must hold and not be arbitrary. What we now call the rule of law—namely, the protection of the rights of individuals and their property—has widened since then, encouraging people to increase their efforts to produce, trade, and innovate. In fact, most economists agree that the rule of law is the single most important factor in explaining the wealth of nations. Without it, there is no incentive to engage in productive economic activities because any commercial success or monetary gain can be expropriated by force.

Much has been done in recent years to focus on how legal governance works, how authority comes to power and is monitored, and the capacity of a country to manage market exchanges. Daniel Kaufmann and his colleagues at the World Bank have examined over two hundred countries, analyzing the process by which those in authority are selected, monitored, and replaced; the government's capacity to effectively manage its resources and implement sound policies; and the respect of citizens for the country's institutions. Rule of law is the institutional infrastructure for a property system that allows commerce to unfold.[4]

There is enormous variation between countries in terms of the composition and operation of the legal environment affecting business. For example, the World Bank studies the complexity and variety of legal systems worldwide, measuring procedural complexity (number of filings, duration, and cost) and variation in employment laws (flexibility of hiring, conditions of employment, and flexibility of firing) to produce an Aggregate Complexity Index.[5] As detailed in table 4-1, the Index shows that Latin America and the Caribbean and Europe and Central Asia have, on average, the most complex legal systems, while South Asia and East Asia have the least complex systems. However, individual country scores range significantly, from a high of 78 for Venezuela to a low of 32 for Canada.

In recent years, political transitions in Eastern Europe and the former Soviet Union, Latin America, Asia, Africa, and the Middle East have all been accompanied by legal reform. These reforms have raised the following questions:

- How do we assess the progress of the reforms?

TABLE 4-1

Legal system complexity

Region/country	Procedural complexity index	Employment laws index	Aggregate complexity index
Latin America and Caribbean	70	61	66
Europe and Central Asia	57	57	57
Middle East and North Africa	59	48	54
South Asia	55	49	52
East Asia and Pacific	55	45	50
Venezuela	81	75	78
Spain	83	70	77
Mexico	62	77	70
Russia	54	79	67
Greece	64	67	66
France	79	50	65
Brazil	48	78	63
Italy	64	59	62
Chile	73	50	62
Poland	65	55	60
Kuwait	76	41	59
Thailand	53	61	57
Germany	61	51	56
Hungary	57	54	56
Saudi Arabia	48	61	55
Egypt	50	59	55
United Arab Emirates	61	45	53
Finland	48	55	52
Belgium	54	48	51
India	50	51	51
South Korea	50	51	51
Czech Republic	65	36	51
Netherlands	46	54	50
China	52	47	50
Taiwan	37	57	47
Turkey	38	55	47
South Africa	56	36	46
Ireland	42	49	46
Israel	51	38	45
Norway	48	41	45
Sweden	44	42	43
Austria	54	30	42
Switzerland	44	36	40
Hong Kong	50	27	39
Japan	39	37	38
Singapore	49	20	35
United States	46	22	34
Malaysia	41	25	33
Australia	29	36	33
Denmark	40	25	33
United Kingdom	36	28	32
Canada	29	34	32

Source: World Bank, 2006.

- How do the reforms affect the costs of doing business?

- How robust are civil and commercial codes and other business legislation?

- Has greater professionalism and independence in the judiciary been achieved?

- Are business crimes and other such offenses punished?

- Conducting business is a crucial form of civil liberty—how does it measure up relative to other human rights?

The answers to the above listed questions shape the way in which business and commerce are conducted. In addition, understanding the answers to those questions is crucial for international portfolio investors and businesspeople as they decide in which markets and locations to deploy capital. The outcomes are real—for individuals and countries.

Direct and Indirect Costs of Legal Opacity

There is a strong relationship between corruption and the effectiveness of a country's legal system. An ineffective legal system is a telltale warning sign in pricing risk for securities, trade, and investment. Lack of strong legal transparency encompasses the following:

- High levels of legal complexity and even confusion with regard to the laws themselves and their intent

- High levels of procedural complexity, with regard to how a law is carried out, characterized by the following:

  - Number of written filings to get a case heard

  - Duration of court proceedings from initial filings to finish

- Cost and requirement of legal counsel

- Need for other types of consultative advice to finish a proceeding

It's no accident that, in the past, limited intellectual property came out of France. While an attractive country and market, it takes more than a decade to resolve a patent case there. By the time your patent case is settled, your product is obsolete. Creditor and minority stockholder rights are also very difficult to secure in France, which retards their debt and structured finance markets and increases their relative cost of capital. Comparative legal studies have shown that civil law countries, such as France, have both the weakest investor protections and the least developed capital markets, especially as compared to common law countries.

Rafael La Porta and his Harvard colleagues have painstakingly documented the institutional and property rights of over fifty countries.[6] They found that the comprehensiveness of the legal rules and the quality of enforcement are key determinants in the depth and breadth of debt and equity financing, as well as in the levels of commerce achieved. Moreover, the overwhelming impact of a low-quality legal system is to distort economic and investment decisions, making the financial system more fragile and ineffective. The result is economic development failure because of restricted domestic growth opportunities, but also because of what economists call "adverse selection"—that is, the projects that are financed are more likely to ultimately fail.

Measuring Legal Opacity

Virtually no company chooses where to locate based on an examination of legal codes and practices. Even so, it's a fool's journey through global markets to be unaware of the risks associated with legal opacity.

Is there a home field advantage that any international business person cannot overcome? How easily can local business partners' sidestep the legal system and make it an insider's game? These questions can be answered by measuring legal opacity.

All business environments have rules, but the credibility of those rules underlies the ability to transact business. Furthermore, the legal system conditions a country's ability to withstand global shocks, the temptation of corruption by government and business officials, and the resources available for market and society building. In this dimension of the Opacity Index, we capture not only the content of the law but the functioning capacity of the legal system.

In crafting an understanding of legal opacity, we address a number of questions that a business person must ask when embarking on commercial activities:

- To what extent are legal procedures subject to political influence or risk?

- Can religious tensions override economic and legal rights of businesses?

- How independent is the judiciary?

- What are the time investments and monetary costs of business legal procedures? Where and why do civil and criminal procedures take too long and cost too much?

- How are creditor and shareholder rights treated?

- What are the risks associated with expropriation, profit repatriation, and payment delay?

The legal Opacity Index measures several fundamental pieces of a country's legal system, including insolvency law codes, the structure of the court system, and religious tensions. For this index, we rely on several existing indices and also analyze several raw data sets.

First, we examine property rights. Utilizing World Bank data, we analyze the full sequence of procedures necessary in a business purchase and what is involved in transferring a property title from a seller to a buyer. Time required for such procedures and costs are both measured. Simplifying rules of commerce enables business partners to conduct their behavior in a way that might reduce the need to use the legal system.

Second, we examine how effectively a country's legal system resolves business disputes and what protection it grants to businesses, investors, and other sources of capital. In analyzing the issues, we rely on surveys of court costs and fees of insolvency practitioners, independent auditors, accountants, lawyers, and the like.

Using these and other factors, we determine a country's degree of judicial independence and assess the legal environment of international capital markets in forty-eight countries, as shown in figure 4-1. The legal Opacity Index allows one to determine the risks—whether real or perceived—associated with a country's legal structures.

Understanding the Role of Enforcement

An institutional environment that makes it difficult to enforce contracts and seize collateral, while making it easy to hide cash flows, makes business difficult, to say the least. Repayment and performance cannot remain arbitrary decisions for commerce to determine. Imperfect enforcement through courts ultimately affects the amount of capital, credit, and repayment funds available. The threat of liquidation is an important incentive for repayment and contract performance in business and inefficiency in enforcing business contracts compromises that incentive. Both the cost of enforcement and the fraction of income or collateral that can be seized when there is a commercial breach has a tremendous effect upon interest rates and overall costs of business.

FIGURE 4-1

Legal structure index 2005

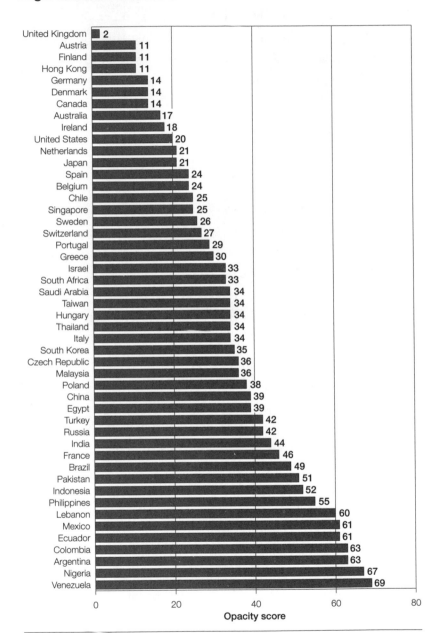

Direct and Indirect Costs of Enforcement Opacity

Enforcement risks often present businesses with a formidable set of challenges. For example, as detailed in the previous chapter, commodities and other goods in some countries do not move without payments to individuals and officials in unions, organized crime, the police, army, or "freelancers" who work the airports, docks, and rail yards. Several factors summarize the economic costs of doing business in a country that has lax enforcement systems. First, the costs associated with organized crime are rolled into our overall cost of enforcement because without proper enforcement, organized crime flourishes. In the port of Odessa, Ukraine, for example, "facilitators" and "customs handlers" work on behalf of their clients by traversing the docks with briefcases filled with cash.[7] Without this money, it is unlikely that cargoes of oil or wheat would make it out of this Black Sea port. Not only does this present business with costs and physical risks, but it also poses a threat given various national laws and OECD conventions which prohibit these payments and other forms of bribes. This category of economic enforcement risk practically defines the "high-frequency" concept discussed earlier, since it is unlikely that any cargo in certain countries would move unless payments are made.

We have also included the economic impacts of terrorism in this category, along with costs related to bureaucratic "red tape" and nontransparent taxation systems. These factors are direct costs because they add to the expense of doing business. But they can also be indirect costs when they simply add to the time it takes to provide goods, capital, or services.

Harvard's La Porta and his team have gone to great lengths to compare what they call "procedural formalism" in a number of countries, and determine how this formalism affects dispute resolution in economic affairs.[8] Procedural formalism comprises a great deal of what we try to capture in looking at the transparency of enforcement in dispute resolution: the extent to which lawyers and judges regiment the steps that disputants follow, how they regulate the collection and presentation of evidence, and how they generally perform in the enforcement of decisions. All of this contributes to a measure of the length of time it takes to resolve disputes. They also add to the direct costs of doing business since high levels of procedural formalism tend to require the use of lawyers and consultants over longer periods and also require a higher level of written submissions, specially prepared collateral material, and expert testimony.

La Porta's body of work is informative and requisite for investment decisions of all sorts. The duration of commercial dispute resolution is very much related to the enforcement of laws, policies, and programs related to economic growth. Where formalism is extensive and there is little judiciary independence, the duration of dispute resolution is quite high and enormous inefficiencies are introduced in the economic process. Moreover, such excessive formalism in legal procedures is related to an overall lower quality of the legal system. The impact of such formalism, transplanted through colonialism to many developing countries, results in extreme costs and delays, unwillingness of economic actors to use courts, and is ultimately associated with more economic injustice and lower growth rates. Judicial and economic reform suggests that the dominance of formalism empowers bureaucracies that respond to noneconomic incentives that distort economic requirements for growth.

Measuring Enforcement Opacity

As discussed, the formal existence of legal rules does not insure their enforcement. Transparency in enforcement decisions is necessary for businesses to understand and predict the law.

As illustrated in figure 4-2, the enforcement score captures the costs, both direct and indirect, of enforcing a contract. The index is

FIGURE 4-2

Enforcement index 2005

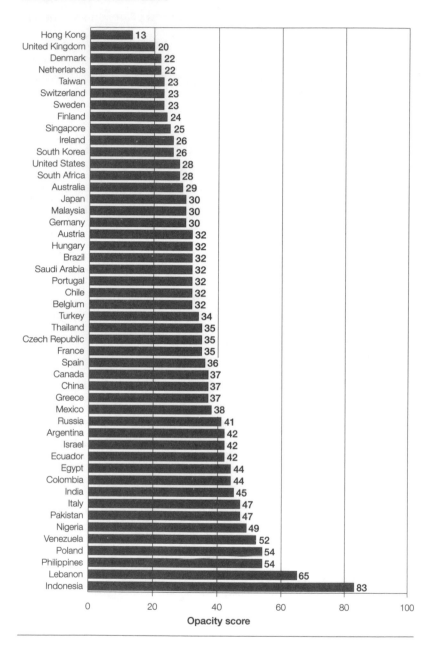

	Opacity score
Hong Kong	13
United Kingdom	20
Denmark	22
Netherlands	22
Taiwan	23
Switzerland	23
Sweden	23
Finland	24
Singapore	25
Ireland	26
South Korea	26
United States	28
South Africa	28
Australia	29
Japan	30
Malaysia	30
Germany	30
Austria	32
Hungary	32
Brazil	32
Saudi Arabia	32
Portugal	32
Chile	32
Belgium	32
Turkey	34
Thailand	35
Czech Republic	35
France	35
Spain	36
Canada	37
China	37
Greece	37
Mexico	38
Russia	41
Argentina	42
Israel	42
Ecuador	42
Egypt	44
Colombia	44
India	45
Italy	47
Pakistan	47
Nigeria	49
Venezuela	52
Poland	54
Philippines	54
Lebanon	65
Indonesia	83

comprised of variables such as average days of legal procedure from filing to enforcement, formalism of contract enforcement, monetary cost of enforcing a contract, cost of organized crime and terrorism, and bureaucratic red tape. Freedom of the press is also a variable we consider in enforcement because a free press environment provides greater public monitoring of judges and public officials.

Case Studies: Legal and Enforcement Opacity Explored

The wide variation in cases of legal and enforcement opacity illustrates just how many types of practices a businessperson might face and how frequently they may have to deal with them.

China's Intellectual Property Battles

In China, a great deal of lip service has been given regarding the eradication of piracy, especially with respect to intellectual property and trademarks.[9] To attract media attention and assert that this time they mean business, Chinese steamrollers have driven over everything from counterfeit jewelry (fake Rolex and Cartier watches, for example) to drugs, fashion items, and bootlegged movies, books, and music albums. During these public displays, solemn statements have been read affirming that China will no longer tolerate piracy. And yet, counterfeit production in the form of fake Prada and Louis Vuitton bags sold on the streets of New York, Paris, Amsterdam, and London still exists. While Chinese officials may be sincere when they express their willingness to prosecute to the fullest each counterfeiter they find, arrests for piracy and counterfeiting are still rare.

While China's counterfeiting industry has been a persistent multibillion dollar problem for businesses for decades, it has taken a new twist that companies must understand and face, especially if they wish to do business there. In what appears to be an effort to support its fledgling, twelve-company pharmaceutical industry, the Chinese State Intellectual Property Organization's (SIPO) Patent Reexamination Board has abrogated some non-Chinese pharmaceutical companies' patent protections.[10]

In 2004, Pfizer Inc., which holds the patent on sildenafil citrate, the main ingredient in Viagra, an erectile dysfunction drug, said that SIPO had overturned its patent on its product. Soon after it decided against Pfizer, SIPO curtailed patent protection for rosiglitazone, a component in one of GlaxoSmithKline's drugs for treating diabetes. Other non-Chinese pharmaceutical companies fear that their patents will be infringed upon as well.

Analysts have said that SIPO's actions against Pfizer and Glaxo-SmithKline go against the rules of the World Trade Organization (WTO), which has set up guidelines, rules, and enforcement procedures to stop piracy. But individual companies cannot successfully rely on the WTO, or other international organizations, when a governmental agency adopts rules that break international conventions; the process is too slow and often ineffective.

China appears to be taking a new strategy. While demonstrating against piracy and counterfeiting, it has in essence made its enforcement and regulatory agencies into the country's chief pirates. China's high opacity scores in the legal realm indicate little recourse for investors whose intellectual assets are taken or harmed. Whereas some countries, like India and South Africa, have ignored patent rights repeatedly in order to bring AIDS drugs to market under the rationale that they are too poor to pay the going rate and are in the midst of an AIDS epidemic, China's rationale seems far more mercenary. It is appropriating patents in order to jumpstart its own pharmaceutical industry.

For China—at least on paper—SIPO's ruling appears to indicate that the country is abandoning piracy in favor of the rule of law. After all, SIPO is a governmental agency whose charter is to protect intellectual property. But seen from a company's point of view, SIPO's mandate makes it more like an agency dedicated to the growth of China's pharmaceutical industry than the unbiased protector of intellectual property. A country's legal machinery is supposed to promote justice, not one industrial group over another.

In the case of SIPO, China is throwing its weight around. The vastness of its markets means that China is gambling that companies like Pfizer prefer losing some of their market and revenue to SIPO-regulated Chinese companies, in lieu of losing the entire market under the old system. Given that SIPO is a regulator and has adopted a strategy of intentional piracy, there is little a foreign company can do except agree to have disputes settled in another jurisdiction, such as low-opacity Hong Kong or Singapore. Such a strategy, however, cannot be implemented after the fact. What China did to books and software—ignored copyrights and pirated them audaciously—and is now doing to pharmaceuticals, it is very likely to do to other industries as well.

The trouble is, however, that as China's twelve pharmaceutical companies grow and become rich, they will be doing it on the basis of someone else's research investment. The long-term prognosis for that kind of approach is grim. Beyond hurting U.S. patent-holder's profits, drug piracy injures consumers. Recent studies estimate that approximately 300,000 people die each year in China due to counterfeit or substandard medicine.[11] Furthermore, what was once a problem isolated to the Chinese population, albeit a major one, is now reaching the U.S. borders: in 2005, customs agents blocked more than fifty shipments of the bird flu drug Tamiflu they believed to be counterfeit. When tested, the drugs had no active ingredients and may have contained illegal chemicals. With Chinese companies beginning to produce parts for Boeing's new 787 jetliner, another industry could very well succumb.

Patents Under Attack in Canada

The Canadian generic drug company Apotex Inc. started shipping its generic version of the anticlotting drug Plavix last August.

For a few weeks in August, the generic version captured nearly three-quarters of the American market for the $6 billion-a-year drug—until Sanofi-Aventis and Bristol-Myers Squibb, the makers of Plavix, asked a judge to halt sales.[12] Following Pfizer's cholesterol-lowering drug Lipitor, Plavix was the second best-selling drug in the world in 2005. Apotex had received approval from the FDA to market its generic version of Plavix in January 2006.

Bristol and Sanofi brought a patent violation suit against Apotex. The companies agreed to settle the case later, with Bristol and Sanofi agreeing to pay Apotex at least $40 million. In return for the payment, Apotex would be allowed to market its generic version of the drug six months before the patent expired in 2011.

In 2004, there were fourteen drug patent validity lawsuits that were settled by agreements among the parties. There were no payments made by the patent holders to the party claiming that the patent was unenforceable. In 2006, at least six of the ten drug patent violation cases resulted in the patent-holding drug company making a "settlement" payment to the generic drug company. In return for the payment, the generic drug company agreed to delay its introduction of its generic version of the drug.[13]

Some Federal Trade Commission officials say that this type of agreement is a restraint of trade and results in higher costs to consumers. Deborah Platt Majoras, chairwoman of the commission, said that she was concerned that payments by brand-name drug companies to the generic drug companies in this type of case may be nothing more than a hidden bribe to the generic company to keep their version of the drug off the market.

Pharmaceutical Problems in Hungary

Other countries have experienced similar troubles in enforcing intellectual property laws. Most frequent are violations of the WTO's Agreement on Trade-Related Aspects of Intellectual Property Rights

(TRIPs), which sets intellectual property standards across member countries. For example, WTO has serious concerns with Hungary's failure to adequately protect confidential test data associated with applications for marketing approval submitted by pharmaceutical companies.[14] Specifically, Hungary does not provide protection against the unfair commercial use of test or other data submitted to its regulatory authorities to obtain marketing approval. As a result, generic pharmaceutical companies have been permitted to rely on data generated and submitted by innovator companies—without their consent—almost immediately after the original application for marketing approval has been filed. The U.S. pharmaceutical industry estimates that it loses between $50 and $100 million annually due to this and other weaknesses in Hungary's data protection regime.

Andean Countries: Failed Obligations

Other countries that do not appear to meet their TRIPS obligations include several countries in the Andean Community, (as well as the Dominican Republic, India, Israel, and Kuwait).[15] Furthermore, many countries fail to provide what the WTO defines as "adequate and effective" intellectual property protection. Bolivia, Colombia, Ecuador, and Peru are examples.[16] Although the four nations currently have bilateral Intellectual Property Rights (IPR) obligations with the United States and international obligations with the WTO, they have failed to provide adequate levels of copyright protection and effective enforcement. This failure has exacerbated the problem and continues to result in significant trade distortions and losses in the Andean region. The economic consequence of this type of opacity is immediate: losses in these countries due to copyright piracy were at least $263 million in 2002 and $256 million in 2006. Copyright law reform alone, without adequate and effective enforcement, does not satisfy the copyright-related commitments made by these governments.

Trouble in Turkey: Initial Failure of the Privatization Campaign

Legal opacity may impede a country's ability to transact business, as was the case with Turkey's privatization campaign in the mid-1980s and early 1990s. After financial difficulties, the IMF persuaded Turkey to begin a privatization program as a means to transition into a market economy. Although it was broadly supported by the legislature, in its early days, the privatization program only approved a small number of Transfer of Operation rights and put several preapproved projects on hold.[17] Given the size of Turkey's state-owned enterprises, it was surprising that the privatization effort had not been more successful. Analysts believe the chief cause of the program's failure was inattention to legal constraints prior to initiation of the privatization program.[18]

Before the privatization program was launched, Morgan Guaranty Bank conducted an assessment of the Turkish legal system to determine if privatization of state-owned enterprises faced legal constraints. While the report found that specific legal changes were necessary to facilitate privatization, it stated that, overall, Turkish law did not prohibit privatization.[19] Rather than identify and resolve these issues of "specific legal changes," the Turkish government proceeded with privatization plans, deeming the changes too time-consuming. As a result, most initial privatization cases were successfully challenged in Turkey's Constitutional Court by opponents of privatization.[20] In an attempt to accelerate privatization, the government issued a series of governmental decrees; however, the legality of these decrees was then challenged by the courts. In 1999, the Parliament amended the Turkish Constitution to allow privatization of public services.[21] Despite this, Turkish privatization efforts continue to experience legal hurdles, harming the financial potential of privatization.

Asian Crisis and Enforcing Contracts: Creditors' Rights

As Barry Eichengreen has pointed out, financial instability arises not simply from formal law, but how law is or is not enforced. During the Asian Crisis of the late '90s, banking, currency, and financial crises were exacerbated not simply because of problems with the design of Indonesia's bankruptcy law, Indonesia's and South Korea's regulatory standards, regulations concerning connected lending, or accounting, but because of how these were inconsistently and arbitrarily enforced. Conflicts of interest, political pressures, corruption, limited administrative capacity, and the absence of an independent judiciary all conspired to disable a financial and business system despite the presence of formal legal systems in each country.

Take the case of bankruptcy laws, which can be opaque and difficult to enforce due to complexity, time, and expense—all direct costs to creditors. Examine what happened in two countries, Thailand and Indonesia, in the wake of the Asian Crisis.

Thailand. Thai Petrochemical Industry (TPI) was a rapidly growing company in the early 1990s.[22] During the Asian Crisis, which began mid-1997, the company suffered extensively from floating of the baht and its subsequent rapid devaluation. The company had greatly increased its debt burden due to its dependency on foreign funds for their expansion. Expansion plans were put on hold while the firm experienced significant losses and struggled to restructure debt and find strategic coinvestment partners. TPI was declared insolvent in a landmark court decision handed down in early 2000, effectively giving creditors control over the rehabilitation and restructuring of the company.

Four years after the initial filing, the case became Thailand's largest and longest-playing bankruptcy case, with the company owing approximately $2.7 billion to creditors. In 2003, the case became twisted when the court allowed the founder of TPI, Prachai

Leophairatana, to resume control of the company. This opaque move ousted the court-appointed debt manager, Effective Planners, because, according to the court, Effective Planners had caused TPI's profits to drop. However, careful examination showed that the profit drop was a result of legal battles brought by Leophairatana against the debt manager throughout the three years Effective Planners controlled the firm.

Most of Leophairatana's lawsuits have been dismissed; the various courts involved indicated their ridiculousness. The firm's major creditors, including Bangkok Bank PCL and Kreditanstalt fuer Wiederaufbau, which are owed approximately $2.7 billion, withdrew as much as $80 million in credit and froze $20 million in assets.

Leophairatana has been viewed as a CEO who dug his own grave through mismanagement of the firm, which grew from a family business to a major Thai company. However, this case may have been managed more effectively if not for the slow and cumbersome legal and enforcement systems. These systems create opacity by making it difficult to follow progress toward an end and understand the criteria by which legal decisions are made. This type of opacity has a chilling effect on foreign investment by making potential investors wary about their options should trouble arise.

Indonesia. Indonesia provided another interesting example of opacity due to procedural complexity. At the end of 1998, Indonesia revised its bankruptcy laws, imposing:

- A deadline of thirty days for court decisions

- A new commercial court with specially trained judges

- Independent receivers for liquidation and administrators for 270-day suspension of payments as an alternative to liquidation and state receivership

- A fast-track enforcement process

However, the deadline was rarely, if ever, enforced, and a shortage of trained accountants and lawyers hampered the resolution system. Debtors stripped assets from companies and transferred them to the subsidiaries' parent companies. As with Thailand, the courts' progress—or lack thereof—was difficult to follow. Cases were dismissed on technical grounds and on average, only five cases were evaluated out of dozens. The investing and ownership class of the country managed to reshuffle the deck to their advantage once again.[23]

Legal Success in the EU: Broadband Pays a Fine in France

Not all legal and enforcement cases end badly. In the case of transparent legal systems like that of the EU Court of First Instance (Europe's second-highest court), the legal system effectively regulates business and investment. Take the case of the French broadband company Wanadoo. In 2003, the European Commission slapped an antitrust fine on France Telecom SA (the owners of Wanadoo) for monopolizing the broadband market.[24] France Telecom retaliated, stating that their prices, which regulators had deemed "predatory," were not illegal, and that they were not monopolizing the European broadband market. However, in early 2007, an EU court upheld the ruling and the fine, to the tune of nearly $13 million. The court found that France Telecom "undercut its rivals," charging prices that did not even cover costs in an attempt to monopolize the market. The "predatory pricing" in question ran from March 2001 to October 2002.

Dealing Strategically with Legal and Enforcement Opacity

What can companies do? While every company that dreams big thinks it needs a BRICs (Brazil, Russia, India, and China) strategy such a strategy requires more than investment. At a minimum, it is vital for globalizing companies to include their legal teams in their strategy sessions. This—sadly and expensively—is rarely done.

In some industries, like pharmaceuticals, the best approach is to use a low opacity country as the entry point, such as Hong Kong in the case of China. Hong Kong, with respect to China, is a better-regulated back door.

In addition, a company can set up a quid pro quo joint venture. For example, a U.S. company might use its Brazilian partner to ease its way into Brazil with the proviso that the Brazilian partner uses its American partner to market its wares in the United States. Without the opportunity to apply a little "reciprocal" pressure on its BRICs counterpart, the American company is likely to find itself with a shrinking share of its target market. Globally minded legal teams that can facilitate such an arrangement must work alongside a company's business strategist. To exclude them from such strategic deliberations could result in unwelcome surprises.

Chapter Five

Accounting Opacity

CHUOAOYAMA, formerly an independent member of the PricewaterhouseCoopers' global network of accounting firms, employs seventeen hundred CPAs and audits fifty-three hundred companies.[1] On September 13, 2005, four ChuoAoyama certified public accounts were arrested by the Tokyo District Public Prosecutors Office on suspicion of violating Securities and Exchange Laws by window-dressing accounts at Kanebo, Ltd., a leading Japanese textile firm.[2] Like Enron in the United States, this case exposed a culture of tolerance about questionable accounting activities: window-dressing became a common "appropriate" activity, despite the conflict of interests engendered by the close relationship between the accounting firm and client. News accounts allege that ChuoAoyama actually engaged in "cooking lessons" for their books.

The ChuoAoyama team had been auditing Kanebo for at least thirty years. Kanebo's accounting showed that it lost money on a consolidated basis due to huge losses in a blanket-making subsidiary. The auditors advised Kanebo's management to reduce its shareholding in the subsidiary and deconsolidate it. They, in turn, would turn a blind eye to the booking of fictitious sales to pad revenue numbers. The irregularity was only discovered after Kanebo, burdened by massive debts, restructured under the government's Industrial Revitalization Corporation.

Understanding Accounting

In 1594, two years after Columbus discovered America and a quarter century after the invention of the printing press, a Franciscan monk name Luca Pacioli published the first text for double-entry bookkeeping. In doing so, he documented a method used by merchants in Venice during the Italian Renaissance. His objective was to "give the trader without delay information as to his assets and liabilities." With industrialization in the nineteenth century, textile and railroad companies further advanced accounting practices. And as multi-divisional firms like DuPont and General Motors sought to keep up with the growing complexity of economic and industrial organization in the 1920s, accounting took yet another leap forward.

Accounting enforcement differs significantly across countries, and is even nonexistent in some places. But research has found a general pattern with respect to the history of a country's legal system. Studies reveal that common-law countries have more timely and standardized accounting and standards enforcement. Nordic code law is associated with increased accounting disclosure, whereas German and French legal systems reduce financial disclosure (relative to common-law countries).[3] But legal standards and background alone do not determine accounting disclosure. More significantly, the structure of concentrated corporate power in a country affects accounting disclosure.Concentration refers to a situation where a small number of firms account for a large proportion of economic activity, such as total sales, employment, and assets. Economic concentration is largely associated with reduced efficiency and performance. In countries with higher ownership concentration where banks can invest directly in companies (for example, Japan), higher concentration of corporate power is associated with reduced public accounting disclosure.

Due to the wide variation in accounting rules across countries, various international organizations have sought to harmonize accounting practices. The International Accounting Standards Committee/Board (IASC/IASB), the International Organization of Securities Commissions (IOSCO), and the World Federation of Exchanges (WFE) actively promote greater disclosure by firms and transparency of financial information.[4]

Accounting Opacity: Tricks and Techniques

Despite these efforts to harmonize and regulate accounting practices, recent high-profile collapses of companies like Maxwell (publishing and media), BCCI (global banking), Polly Peck (textiles), and others late in the twentieth century have highlighted the number of techniques developed in recent years to distort accounting practices and reporting.[5] All involve overstating or understating income, cheating vendors, falsifying documents, and inflating numbers through the companies' financial reporting systems. In addition to the tricks outlined below, opaque accounting practices can also include understatement of liabilities, revenue recognition, purchase accounting, and manipulated restatements. These patterns vary across country depending on other aspects of opacity and the ability of legal, enforcement, and regulatory applications to limit these abuses.

Round-tripping. Trades between energy, telecommunications, or other similar companies, wherein two trading companies essentially swap the same amount of energy or service for the same price, are called round-tripping, also known as wash trades. The trades inflate a company's revenue and trading volumes but appear to serve no other economic purpose. Traders and analysts say the practice is also used to manipulate energy markets by setting up bogus benchmark prices or creating artificial market liquidity for sometimes lightly traded energy contracts. Some companies that have engaged in these trades say they serve legitimate business purposes such as verifying current market prices.

Laddering. Laddering occurs when underwriters allocate shares in the aftermarket at increasingly higher prices. This artificially inflates stock prices by enabling underwriters and issuers to earn huge profits: they buy at the initial public offering (IPO) price and sell at inflated prices. As a result, underwriters offer hot IPO's to investors who promise to buy greater amounts of stock and receive kickbacks through undisclosed commissions.

Stuffing. Stuffing refers to improper revenue recognition and the accounting abuse that derives from it. Companies will "stuff" the distribution channel by shipping larger-than-normal volumes of goods at the end of a reporting period and booking the revenue without acknowledging possible returns. Other related methods include "bill and hold," consignment sales, overestimation of revenue under the percentage of completion method, recognition of revenue for defective products, and premature recognition of revenue.

Accounting Opacity in the Internet Age and Beyond

Accounting opacity faces new challenges and concerns with the collapse and revival of the internet economy since the turn of the twenty-first century. E-commerce companies and projects face tremendous tests in transparency of reporting. During the period of explosive growth, e-companies largely focused on growing revenue rather than profits. This influenced budgeting, project selection, and compensation decisions, creating a minefield of moral hazard as executives tried to justify overvalued stock prices through unprofitable acquisitions or marked-up revenues.

Brand recognition (like eBay), patents (like Priceline), and supplier relations (like Dell) don't create anything tangible, so expenditures to acquire them are not recognized as investments by Generally Accepted Accounting Principles (GAAP), a set of guidelines for financial accounting.[6] The debate on capitalizing or expensing customer acquisition or R&D expenses has a long history. The case for capitalizing R&D can be made in the following ways:

- Expensing may have been reasonable when it was negligible as a proportion of total cost, but in technology-driven businesses it can be significant.

- Expensing understates corporate profits and therefore overstates price/earnings ratios.

- Insiders at technology firms make higher profits from insider sales because expensing hides their value from the public.

- Inconsistency in accounting applications makes it difficult to compare firms in the same business.

The Financial Accounting Standards Board (FASB) justifies expensing for three reasons:

- Future benefits of these expenditures are uncertain.

- Benefits can't be objectively measured.

- A causal relationship between current R&D and/or marketing expenses has not been demonstrated.[7]

As Shivaram Rajgopal at the University of Washington has shown, there is substantial economic evidence about the relationship between intangible expenditures (for example, R&D or marketing) and both future earnings and share value.[8] These controversies riddled the financial scandals earlier this decade as companies have moved from managing earnings to manipulating them. But these issues threaten very legitimate companies in biotech and other technology sectors as well.

Measuring Accounting Opacity

Accounting opacity relates not simply to fraud, but to the ways that accounting manipulation can become impermeable to detection by technically operating legally, yet confounding and confusing all aspects of market disclosure. During the Enron scandal, which eradicated forty-five hundred jobs and wiped out over $70 billion in investors' equity,[9] an Enron accountant provided a story, "Dog versus Duck," that perfectly describes what we mean: you've got a dog, and for accounting purposes you need it to be a duck. So, you slap a yellow beak on its nose, put some feathers on it and web feet on its paws. Then you say, "Look, it's a duck, because it meets all the accounting requirements of what a duck is." But you know it's still a dog. This difference between calling things what they are in the real world and simply following procedures is key to what we try to capture in measuring accounting opacity.

The accounting Opacity Index captures the strength of accounting reporting standards of each country, as shown in figure 5-1. It is constructed of ten questions that indicate a country's practice regarding general accounting standard disclosures, general recognition and measurements, recognition of financial assets, disclosure of ownership, corporate governance guidelines, and auditing requirements. We examine accounting opacity in terms of the quality of accounting standards and the enforcement and corporate application of those standards.

Several specific items are included in the index in order to pinpoint accounting enforcement as it relates to evaluating country differences and gaining a clear view into company operations. These include:

- *Audit spending:* Higher levels of spending on external auditing are associated with stronger audit firms and closer compliance with audit standards. In research literature, this is measured by the total fees of a country's ten largest auditing firms as a percentage of GDP.

FIGURE 5-1

Accounting index 2005

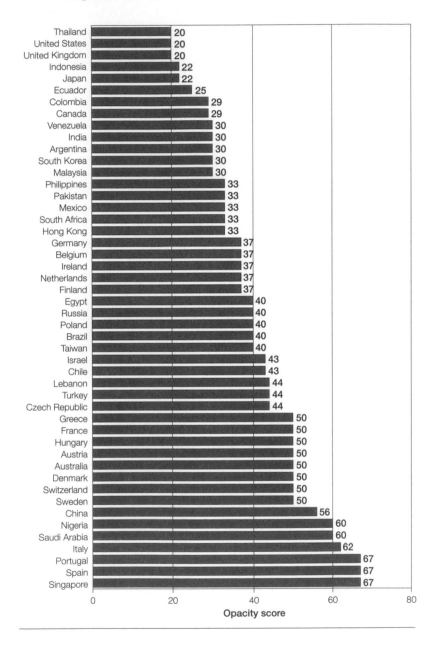

- *Insider trading laws:* Insider trading laws may deter managers from manipulating earnings to profit from trading in a firm's stock. Insider trading laws exist in 87 of 103 countries with securities laws, but prosecutions have occurred in only 38 countries.

- *Stronger shareholder protection:* These protections limit management's manipulation of financial reporting of earnings. The mechanisms by which shareholders can sue directors for losses incurred due to manipulated financial reports are more plentiful in some countries than in others— for example, more plentiful in the United States than in Germany.

Overall, the United Kingdom, Sweden, Finland, and Germany have lower scores, indicating that accounting disclosure and transparency is best in these countries. The United States, United Kingdom, and Canada tend to enforce accounting standards more systematically, while countries like Spain and Italy do not. These findings follow general research on accounting opacity.

Case Studies: Recent Lessons in Accounting Opacity

Accounting underlies the ultimate resolution of opacity problems as it is directly connected to clarity of information concerning business operations and investments. *The Smartest Guys in the Room*, a recent documentary about the Enron scandal, highlights this point.[10] In the Enron case, the problem was not merely accounting fraud, but that complex business and accounting rules were explicitly bent. Ultimately, because the accounting opacity was so high, this scandal destroyed Arthur Andersen, one of the country's most respected accounting firms.

We now explore other cases where accounting opacity has had similar destructive results.

Accounting Disasters in Japan

Accounting opacity has struck Japan in several key areas, from traditional industries, like textiles, to banking and the fragile technology industry. We opened this chapter with a case study of Japanese accounting firm ChuoAoyama. In addition to its troubles with the textile firm Kanebo, ChuoAoyama also faced trouble for audits of Ashikaga Bank, a large regional bank.[11] Ashikaga Bank was nationalized in 2003 after the Financial Services Agency (FSA), Japan's financial regulator, found that the bank had fiddled its accounts to hide insolvency. As a result of this and other scandals, on May 10, 2006, the FSA imposed an unprecedented penalty: ChuoAoyama was barred from doing business for two months. Despite the seemingly short period, ChuoAoyama was still badly hurt because Japanese law requires auditors to cancel contracts with clients if their business has been suspended.

Japan's technology industry has also been adversely affected. After two years of investigation, Japanese authorities found that officers of the internet start-up Livedoor Marketing had padded their parent company's profits.[12] Furthermore, they had released false information during Livedoor's takeover of Money Life in 2004: they had filed falsified revenue statements that overstated earnings and engaged in insider trading and money laundering.

Proposals for accounting and auditing reform in Japan have been discussed for some time. These range from cutting the intimate ties between auditors and their clients by requiring rotation and longer intervals between renewals to extending criminal charges to include accounting companies, not just the employees, who pad accounts.

Accounting Troubles in Russia's Transitioning Economy

The problems of accounting opacity have been apparent in transition economies as well. Banking crises in the Czech Republic, Hungary, and Poland have all been associated with reporting rule problems.[13] In particular, the transition from state to public ownership in Russia has been rife with accounting problems.[14]

The case of Hermitage Capital Management, a minority shareholder in Russia's state-controlled Gazprom (with over $20 billion in annual sales and the world's largest reserves of natural gas), illustrates this problem.[15] Hermitage Capital Management sued Gazprom and its international auditor, Pricewaterhouse Coopers (PWC), when it discovered that PWC had incentives to hide company performance. Hermitage tracked a number of transactions between Gazprom and the Russian gas company, Itera. They noted that assets were "airlifted" (that is, transferred at a negligible price) out of Gazprom and into another entity, depressing Gazprom's stock price in the market. Hermitage complained that PWC "had huge incentives to co-operate with the management and say everything was okay and no disincentives in the form of lawsuits and regulations for them not to."

Gazprom was the latest in a long list of companies with dubious accounting methods in Russia. Similar scandals have occurred in telecommunications, mining, and manufacturing, renewing calls for accounting reform and outside evaluation of directors.

Another case of transition economy problems with opacity in Russia relates to its relationship with multilateral organizations, such as the International Monetary Fund (IMF). On March 16, 2001, the *Financial Times* reported that Swiss prosecutors were investigating the alleged misappropriation of $4.8 billion that the International Monetary Fund (IMF) lent to Russia in July 1998, shortly before Russia's default in August.[16] This and other cases in Russian's transition (such as the Gazprom case highlighted above), demonstrated failure by the IMF and international accounting firms to construct accurate, comprehensive balance sheets of Russia's commercial banks and the Central Bank of Russia. Apparently, prior to the default that created substantial systemic risk in the global financial system, the Central Bank of Russia had moved beyond the boundaries of "creative accounting" to actually misreporting reserves to sustain the ruble.

The purpose of the IMF loans was to prop up the banking system (especially SBS-Agro) and the ailing ruble. Instead, these and other funds ended up in the bank accounts of obscure corporations and then vanished. The Audit Chamber of the Russian Duma eventually reported that the Central Bank was selling dollars for rubles and extending ruble loans to a few well-connected commercial banks, thus subsidizing their dollar purchases. Rubles were printed by the Central Bank to fund this lucrative arbitrage. The dollars were from the IMF. Roughly $50 billion in transfers of the nation's hard currency reserves were transferred from the Central Bank to the Financial Management Company (FIMACO) of the Channel Islands. FIMACO was majority-owned by Eurobank, the Central Bank's Parisian-based subsidiary, which was 23 percent owned by Russian companies and private individuals. FIMACO used these funds to fuel the speculative government Treasury Bill (GKO) market. It disbursed nonreported profits to "trust companies" of Russian citizens and institutions, becoming a large slush fund for patronage.

The IMF later concluded that "capital transferred abroad from Russia may represent legal activities as exports, or illegal sources. But it is impossible to determine whether specific capital flows from Russia—legal or illegal—come from a particular inflow, such as IMF loans or export earnings."[17] It is important to note how opacity in multilateral financial institutions has possibly fueled persistent problems in transition economies.

Accounting Opacity Transcends Boundaries in the Netherlands

The Ahold case represents how accounting opacity transcends boundaries.[18] Ahold, the troubled Dutch food retail group, announced the results of an investigation into the accounts at its U.S. Foodservice arm in 2004. The pattern of accounting distortion transcended national boundaries: it occurred in the United States, Chile, Poland, the Czech Republic, and Scandinavia as Ahold sought to cover losses in Latin America through transfer payments and other accounting distortions. Profit overstatements mushroomed from $500 million to $800 million after examination. The company was required not only to dismiss those involved in the fraud, but to embark on a program of divestments throughout Latin America and Asia as it attempted to defensively consolidate back to its European base.

Ahold escaped strong punishment because the Netherlands does not have a strong regulating body like the SEC. Restatements were due to legal, yet questionable practices like "claiming profits of acquired firms as 'organic growth,' booking capital gains from sale and lease-back deals as profit, and keeping billions of dinar demoninated debt off its balance sheet."[19]

A Positive Turn: New Standards in China

Not all accounting news is bad news. China made a big move this year in reforming its accounting system. The Ministry of Finance announced in January 2007 that the twelve hundred companies listed on the Shenzhen and Shanghai stock markets will be required to adopt, with important exceptions, norms similar to the International Financial Reporting Standards (IFRS).[20]

The new accounting system will certainly help China achieve greater transparency, which should lead not just to better economic management, but also to a freer society. This shift, however, is easy to announce and hard to carry through. Two of the obstacles to implementation are much discussed: a shortage of experienced accountants and the lack of deep financial markets. The third, a deep-seated fear in China, is that the government and its companies will punish anyone who complains through quiet blacklisting. And the new accounting standards will not work unless people criticize and complain.

Martin Fahy, director of development for the Asia-Pacific region at the Chartered Institute of Management Accounts said, "You can't have a functioning financial market and economy without objective and independent accounting. This is a test for not only China, but for the integrity of the accounting profession as well."[21]

Dealing Strategically with Accounting Opacity

Accounting opacity matters because, insofar as a country or firm is committed to greater disclosure, lowered opacity risks should lower the costs of capital that arise from information asymmetries.

There are real economic consequences to accounting opacity. If accounting is opaque, firm shares become less liquid. Investors demand a higher discount for holding shares in illiquid markets, resulting in fewer proceeds and a higher cost of capital. As countries and firms increase their disclosures, the subsequent information gaps between firms and shareholders, buyers and sellers reduce this discount and lower the cost of capital.

As research related to the components of our index shows, firms and countries that elect internationally accepted reporting requirements (International Accounting Standards or US-GAAP), rather than adopting local accounting standards, reflect increased levels of accounting disclosure, leading to real economic gains. Studies that have examined bid-ask spreads, trading volume, and share price volatility confirm the positive impact of less opacity in accounting standards.

The variation between international accounting standards and local ones suggests that a shift toward international standards improves measurement and information content. The shift also evidences a commitment to global standards and to the requirements of a more transparent marketplace. When firms commit to reducing accounting opacity, their host countries receive economically and statistically significant benefits by lowering capital costs.

Chapter Six

Regulatory Opacity

I N 1999, FOLLOWING the international crisis and a 3 percent fall in GDP, Argentina entered fully into recession.[1]
President Fernando de la Rúa, who took office in December 1999 after Carlos Menem's ten-year administration, sponsored tax increases
and spending cuts to reduce the deficit, which had ballooned to 2.5
percent of GDP. The new government also arranged a $7.4 billion
stand-by facility with the International Monetary Fund (IMF) for
contingency purposes—almost three times the size of Argentina's
previous arrangement.[2] They passed laws intended to change the
country's labor code, and attempted to address the precarious financial situation of several highly indebted provinces by consolidating
debt at the federal level.

But as the year went on, Argentina's massive public debt became a
subject of considerable controversy, and increased tension between
the Argentine government and the IMF. In 2001, capital flight increased and the government found itself unable to meet debt payments. The crisis exploded when an almost complete freezing of bank

deposits, known as the *corralito*, caused massive public protests and rioting in December 2001. President De la Rúa resigned shortly after the riots.

On December 23, 2001, interim president Adolfo Rodríguez Saá declared a short-lived debt moratorium. A few days later, Argentina officially defaulted on $93 billion of its debt. Argentina had failed to pay before, but this time it registered the largest sovereign default in history. The debt restructuring process was long and complex. Argentina offered a steep discount on its obligations (approximately 70 percent) and finally settled the matter with over 76 percent of its defaulted creditors. This default did not include the IMF, which has continued to be paid over time.

In December 2005, Argentine President Néstor Kirchner, elected in mid-2003, decided to liquidate the Argentine debt to the IMF in a single payment, without refinancing, for a total of $9.81 billion.[3] The payment was partly financed by Venezuela, who bought Argentine bonds for $1.6 billion. In May 2006, Argentina reentered international debt markets selling $500 million of its Bonar V five-year dollar-denominated bonds with a yield of 8.36 percent, mostly to foreign banks. Moody's Investors Service boosted Argentina's debt rating from B– to B.

It is generally agreed that the banks held a share of the blame for the situation that led to the corralito. In mid-2001, it was probably clear to bank owners and high-ranking officials that Argentina's banking system was going to crash. In fact, some may have spurred this outcome by informing their highest deposit holders of the imminent crash. These mostly large companies quickly moved their deposits abroad. Meanwhile, banks recommended that their middle-class customers continue to make deposits.

In the end, it is believed that the corralito ended up being good business for some international banks. These banks negotiated with the Argentine government to receive compensation bonds for their "missing" money when, in reality, a large proportion had never really left their banks but had only moved from one branch to another. Regulatory opacity enabled the continuation of weak fiscal policies, which left the Argentine economy vulnerable. The convertibility plan locked in overvaluation, reducing flexibility in the domestic economy. All of these factors converged to create a regulatory environment that sustained the country's unsustainable debt dynamics and enabled capital flight through the bank-enabled restructuring. After more than nine bailouts and extensions of IMF loans since 1983, none of the measures instituted in the context of poor economic policy and political instability addressed the issues of regulatory opacity; indeed, they were enabled by it. The absence of conditionality measures (when a country makes commitments to economic and financial policy) tied to international assistance and debt restructuring perpetuated the flaws in existing financial institutions, their management, and their relationships rather than transformed them. Effective conditionality should have resulted in measures to reduce government spending and deficits, reducing the rate of money growth, reforming the banking sector, and a range of monetary and economic policies that might have more adequately overcome the fiscal breakdown that ensued. The stunning unraveling of the Argentine economy reflects the regulatory and legal frameworks that enabled corruption and other aspects of opacity.

Understanding Regulation

How can corporate strategy understand, engage, and manage regulatory processes and risks? Regulatory opacity is important for several reasons, all related to the ability of an economy and the actors within it—investors, entrepreneurs, workers, managers—to adapt to technological changes and economic growth. Excessive and opaque regulation can lead to inflexibility in labor and capital markets, which stifles mobility and growth for factors of production. Microeconomic inflexibility in firms' finances from both external and internal sources hampers an economy's ability to absorb shock, requiring firms to reallocate resources. This was clear in the financial crises of Asia, Latin America, and Russia in the 1990s and was shown dramatically in the Argentine crisis of 2001–2002.[4] The inability to access capital debt and equity markets to establish more flexible capital structures led to many business failures.

How a firm manages its capital structure to allocate cash flows to various needs and investors can vary enormously. Flexibility in capital and labor markets is critical to navigating through external shocks or changes in corporate strategy or in the global economy. Barriers to firm creation, destruction, restructuring, and transformation are all regulatory issues that can negatively affect a firm's ability to adapt in order to change and grow. They can result in market rules that restrict, rather than enhance, competition. The result, in these cases, is to entrench management and restrict entry of new technologies and firms.

On the other hand, regulations that facilitate change and protect various economic actors can positively affect production factor allocation, capital allocation, competition, and innovation. Investors' rights regulations, protection of foreign investors, creditor rights, and transparency in financial reporting are important to represent adequately to investors. Regulations that facilitate change and protect various economic actors can positively affect production factor allocation, capital allocation, competition, and innovation.

Regulation of goods, services, and factors affecting production has a long and sometimes questionable history. Superficially, regulation is enacted to serve explicit goals that structure the marketplace, with the express purpose of engendering more rational and organized operations. But while it might have a specific social purpose, such as consumer health and safety or employment protection, closer reflection reveals a complex process in a country's political economy whereby legitimate social goals are confounded by the objectives of particular political interest groups seeking to entrench their power.

That is, public regulation is often shaped by private interest. Under these circumstances, regulation often restricts competition rather than increasing it.

The Relationship Between Opacity and Regulation

The relationship between regulation and opacity is not an explicitly direct or indirect one, as it largely is for other CLEAR factors. In order to decrease regulatory opacity overall, regulations that increase reporting and transaction transparency (for example, governance-related regulations) need to be increased, while those regulations that can restrict competition and entry into markets (largely found in business and product regulation) need to be reduced. Hence, analyzing regulatory opacity is more complicated since it requires understanding the content of regulations that enhance or reduce competition and efficiency in the economy as a whole.

Outcomes of Changes in Regulatory Structure

Regulatory structures can promote efficiency and cohesion between financial markets and the private sector, and help countries avoid the widespread disruptions to economic and social welfare that can arise from market failures. Therefore, business dynamics and, ultimately, economic performance depend heavily upon effective and transparent regulation. Countries with better corporate governance create regulations that improve business conditions, as illustrated by the following:

- As a country increases its business and product regulation above the global median, the annual rate of per capita GDP growth decreases by 0.4 percent. If a developing country were to decrease its product market regulation, its annual growth rate would rise about 1.3 percent annually.

- If regulatory governance is improved to levels of the United States, the United Kingdom, or other high-standard regulatory environments, a significant positive impact on economic growth will occur.

- A reduction of product market regulation in developing countries would decrease their economic volatility by over 30 percent.

Regulatory Opacity and Capture

The fusion of public and private interests is often embodied in the intermingling of industry, finance, and public sector. This fusion creates a regulatory environment that encourages a high level of cronyism and organized corruption as accepted behavior. In the wake of the Asian, Mexican, and Russian financial crises, a great deal of research was published examining the prevalence of conglomerate structures of major industries with narrow capital bases.[5] These structures, originally designed to keep control within family or close-held groups, made the overall country vulnerable to financial shocks. In Indonesia, for example, the central bank and the financial restructuring authority channeled over $60 million through an insolvent bank and a front company to the ruling party. In the Former Soviet Union, a Russian oligarch controlling a network of mining, energy, and banking interests exerted considerable influence over the Kremlin and regional governments. As a result, regulatory policies were tailored to his private interests.

These cases, among many others, represent how private influence over the public sphere results in state or regulatory "capture," whereby government agencies come under the influence of the industries they are designed to regulate. This enables individuals and/or industrial groups to influence the formulation of laws and regulations for specific special advantages.

Regulatory Rigidities Vary Around the World

Regions vary greatly in their regulations for business entry, growth, and exit. While all governments oversee and extract revenues from business activities, the variation in regulatory oversight is enormous. Norman Loayza of the World Bank demonstrates this in his research of regulations in industrial versus developing nations.[6] He found that industrial countries tend to adopt heavy fiscal regulation, medium labor regulation, and low regulation in trade, financial markets, entry, bankruptcy, and contract enforcement. However, this pattern varies significantly in developing countries. For example, labor regulation is significantly lower in East Asia and the Pacific, but much higher in Latin America and the Caribbean. On the other hand, trade regulations are generally higher, particularly in the Middle East and North Africa. Some of the harshest and least transparent regulatory systems are in Africa, Iran, and the Philippines.

Direct and Indirect Costs of Regulatory Opacity

The impacts of regulatory opacity upon price and monetary behavior, corporate governance, and entrepreneurial growth in a nation's economy are measurable. Forgone growth, increased inequality, and financial instability are easily exacerbated by patterns of regulatory distortion in the markets. The following sections describe several key areas that are impacted by regulatory opacity.

Negative Impact on GDP Growth

Empirical economic research has extensively examined the impacts of various kinds of regulatory opacity on the key determinants of GDP growth: productivity, investment, and employment. Product market regulations cover:

- State control of business enterprises

- Legal and administrative barriers to entrepreneurship

- Barriers to international trade and investment

This type of misguided regulation lowers productivity growth and has a negative effect on innovation and private investment in the economy of nations. On the other hand, increased product market competition encouraged by deregulation was found to raise both investment and employment. Deregulation in product markets simplifies business rules, thereby making transactions and exchanges in the marketplace more easily accessible to a larger number of market players.

Negative Impact on Labor Markets and Entrepreneurship

Labor regulation studies found that regulations restricting hiring and firing had negative impacts upon employment creation in European and Latin American economies, limiting growth and mobility and negatively affecting job creation. Increased levels and complexity of oftentimes contradictory regulation make labor markets more inefficient and costly. Business regulations also impact firms at every stage—entry, growth, and exit—of their life cycle. Entrepreneurs must follow procedures of varying complexity to start and operate a firm in the arenas of hiring and firing workers, taxes, safety standards, environmental regulations, interest rate controls, trade barriers, legal procedures, financial reporting, and so forth. Closing down or shifting businesses can similarly be encumbered by different types of rules. The increased complexity of rules in business formation or liquidation results in more arbitrary application and vulnerability to political influence, thereby creating greater levels of opacity.

Negative Impact on Governments

The governance problems associated with the absence of regulatory transparency, which results from complex, undisclosed, and restricted information, are widely demonstrated in examining financial regulatory bodies. For example, in studies of the incidence of government ownership of banks, Rafael La Porta showed that there were a number of problems apparent across countries:

- Lower overall quality of government (that is, greater intervention in the economy, lower efficiency, less legal security, more financial crises and associated costs)

- More restricted political rights

- Worse bureaucratic performance and, subsequently, higher corruption

- Slower productivity growth and financial development subsequent to state intervention into bank ownership

- Misallocation of resources (a lower proportion of credit allocated to firms outside the top twenty firms, higher interest rate spreads)

- Lower overall economic growth[7]

Negative Impact on the Cost of Money (Financial Repression)

An underappreciated facet of government action in financial markets around the world is called "financial repression," referring to a variety of means whereby the state, via regulatory intervention, interferes with the free flow of resources from savers to borrowers and represses the growth of capital formation in the entrepreneurial sector. It takes place in numerous forms, all of which "distort" the allocation of resources in society and increase the growth of government relative to the private sector. Financial repression takes the burden off of one favored sector of society and places it on another. Its aim—so we are told—is the common good, which is to say growth. Its impact is not always that clear.

There are both theoretical and practical reasons for financial repression. The most important reason governments engage in financial repression is very simple: it provides additional avenues of financing. The answer to the question of who benefits is clear: the state gains because it is able to channel resources either toward its own fiscal priorities (government programs) or to sectors, firms, or individuals who have the favor of the political apparatus.

Who loses? Primarily, everyone who is prevented from lending and investing in the private sector and obtaining the type of risk-return profile that they desire for their investments. In addition, the forced provision of resources directed by the state denies funding to ventures that would otherwise have received financing (those with good ideas but who do not have the favor of the government), so entrepreneurs may be "crowded out" of capital markets as well. The resulting lack of innovation hurts all consumers indirectly.

Financial repression will end as countries adopt clear, transparent, credible, and predictable rules by which investment policy decisions are made. The end of financial repression will permit easier attainment of innovative ideas and methods for achieving these other goals. The costs of opacity in financial regulatory systems (which makes financial repression possible) are becoming increasingly apparent.[8]

Negative Impact on the Regulation of Financial Activities

Despite variations in trade, labor, and other regulatory areas, many countries have made strides in strengthening bank supervision and regulation on an international level, particularly since the Asian/Russian financial crises of 1997–1998. The Basel Committee on Banking Supervision provides a forum for regular cooperation on banking supervisory matters.[9] It has developed increasingly into a standard-setting body on all aspects of banking supervision, including the Basel II regulatory capital framework.[10] The Committee's members come from Belgium, Canada, France, Germany, Italy, Japan, Luxembourg, the Netherlands, Spain, Sweden, Switzerland, the United Kingdom, and the United States. Countries are represented by their central bank or, in cases where the central bank does not supervise the banking business, by the authority with formal responsibility for banking business.

Despite the Basel Committee's efforts, a wide variation in the regulation of financial activities remains. And with this variation come a number of negative consequences:

- *Conflicts of interest:* Most regulations have tried to prevent conflicts of interest, but an unintended consequence is that several actually *promote* them, especially when banks take on diverse activities. For example, banks might "dump" securities on ill-informed investors or shift risk to assist firms with outstanding loans.

- *Moral hazard:* Moral hazards arise when a person or institution who engages in problematic or immoral behavior causes a problem but doesn't suffer the full (or any) consequences—or in some cases actually benefits. This has occurred when regulations encourage riskier behavior, such as in the Asian Financial Crisis or other banking crises around the world.

- *Financial concentration:* Regulations sometimes allow aggregation of functions to create extremely large and complex entities that are difficult to monitor. The resulting obfuscation of financial operations and creation of institutions and market-players that are too big to discipline reduces competition and efficiency, thus increasing regulatory opacity.

- *Political lending:* Sometimes, governments use financial regulation to promote politically motivated lending. Political or policy lending can be imposed by regulations which then, without accompanying fiscal or monetary policy enabling credit expansion, actually distort credit allocation and the credit cycle. Administratively determining credit allocation thereby raises overall costs of financing for the economy as a whole.

Measuring Regulatory Opacity

The regulatory Opacity Index explores the regulatory environment of international capital markets in forty-eight countries to determine the risks—whether real or perceived—associated with a country's regulatory structures. The regulatory opacity score for these countries is illustrated in figure 6-1.

In measuring regulatory opacity, we are concerned with the following questions: Can investors get a clear understanding of the companies in which they invest, and are there mechanisms to settle disputes arising out of the investment process? Are governance, business, and product regulations complex, obfuscatory, and contradictory? Can new entrants operate on a level regulatory playing field of business competition with established industries? Are regulations protective of established business institutions and their management or competition and market dynamics? In addition to these issues, broadly speaking, we were concerned with how well the countries we studied conformed to the robust regulatory practices that are in use in countries like the United Kingdom and the United States, which have very large capital markets that are, for the most part, well run.

The regulatory Opacity Index is comprised of twenty-four objective indicators of regulatory structures. Data was obtained from leading national and international sources, including central banks, national securities agencies, the Heritage Foundation, the World Bank, the World Economic Forum, International Country Risk Guide, and the *International Securities Services Association Handbook*. As standard protocol, official published figures from primary sources were used wherever possible.

FIGURE 6-1

Regulatory index 2005

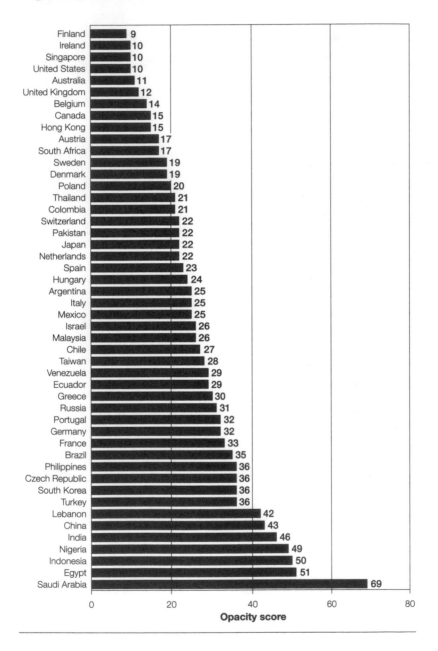

Country	Opacity score
Finland	9
Ireland	10
Singapore	10
United States	10
Australia	11
United Kingdom	12
Belgium	14
Canada	15
Hong Kong	15
Austria	17
South Africa	17
Sweden	19
Denmark	19
Poland	20
Thailand	21
Colombia	21
Switzerland	22
Pakistan	22
Japan	22
Netherlands	22
Spain	23
Hungary	24
Argentina	25
Italy	25
Mexico	25
Israel	26
Malaysia	26
Chile	27
Taiwan	28
Venezuela	29
Ecuador	29
Greece	30
Russia	31
Portugal	32
Germany	32
France	33
Brazil	35
Philippines	36
Czech Republic	36
South Korea	36
Turkey	36
Lebanon	42
China	43
India	46
Nigeria	49
Indonesia	50
Egypt	51
Saudi Arabia	69

Opacity score

The indicators can be further categorized into two broad areas—financial sector and business procedure—which cover key facets of regulatory issues. The financial sector indicators measure the effectiveness of regulations that allow for the efficient operation of financial markets and international transactions as they pertain to private sector development. These indicators comprise seventeen of the twenty-four variables and were drawn from eight sources. Questions considered in this category include:

- Which government agency handles the issuance and settlement of public debt, systems of public debt distribution, and capital flow restrictions?

- Is there a central clearinghouse of settlements if debt is held at a central depository?

- What are the regulations and associated disclosure standards for brokers?

- What are the standards for regulatory and supervisory agencies and what is their degree of independence?

The business procedure indicators gauge the regulatory costs associated with private sector ventures. These seven indicators were obtained from the World Bank "Doing Business" survey and include the number of procedures, length of time, and relative capital necessary to start and close a business.[11] The regulatory structures index provides insight into the multifaceted dimensions of regulatory opacity and ways to assess the relative performance and structures of countries.

Case Studies: Recent Lessons in Regulatory Opacity

In this section, we review the ways that regulatory opacity echoes throughout the business process by delving into a few countries that were faced with significant challenges in this arena. We examine the means and methods of taxation, industrial regulation, and other areas where the unpredictability of regulatory processes has a significant impact on returns.

Arbitrary Taxation as a Form of Regulatory Opacity: The Cases of Mexico and Peru

Regulatory opacity spans from the federal to the local level. However, local governance is where the most arbitrary application of rules can occur. In Guadalcazar, Mexico, the local city council effectively expropriated the property of a U.S. investor, Metalclad, despite the fact that the company had secured federal permits and entitlements for a hazardous waste facility.[12] The local government was able, at least temporarily, to usurp federal powers and send Metalclad into Chapter 11 reorganization. Eventually, with the support of NAFTA provisions, Metalclad recovered $16.5 million plus interest, but the business disruption and failure were irreversible. Clearly, the ability of the local government to preempt earlier federal regulations was an attribute of the regulatory environment unrevealed to investors.

Many tax authorities are also famous for arbitrary tax imposition. The tax authority of the Peruvian Government has frequently violated legal contracts signed with various U.S. companies and unlawfully or retroactively changed tax assessments.[13] Even when Peruvian courts have overturned these actions, the Peruvian government and tax authority have circumvented their rulings and used the appeals process. A Section 527 Report to Congress on Expropriation Claims and Certain Other Investment Disputes lists twelve active investment disputes in Peru that are being handled by local Peruvian authorities.[14] Companies include: Doe Run Company, Duke Energy International, Global Crossing, PSEG Global and Sempra Energy, and the Engelhard Corporation.

In the case of the Engelhard Corporation, in 1999, Engelhard purchased Peruvian gold at fair market prices, paid the value-added tax (VAT) required under Peruvian law, and exported the gold to its U.S. refinery, thereby becoming eligible for a VAT refund. Engelhard's transactions were found to be legal and appropriate by three independent audits, including one performed by Peruvian court-appointed auditors. However, the Government of Peru's position was to hold Engelhard accountable for VAT shortfalls, regardless of what company was ultimately found responsible for the shortfall. The Peruvian Government seized over $30 million in Engelhard assets and tax refunds, producing no evidence—either documentary or testimonial—of any wrongdoing on the part of the company or its officials.

On May 9, 2003, Engelhard filed an action in Peru's Constitutional Court, claiming the Peruvian tax authority had violated the company's rights. On April 28, 2004, the Constitutional Court ruled that Engelhard's rights had, indeed, been violated. The ruling implicitly and repeatedly stated that Engelhard cannot be held responsible for the actions of third parties.[15] The ruling further stated that the documentary evidence filed by SUNAT did not demonstrate any irregularities in the purchase of gold by Engelhard. The Court also ruled that the Peruvian government violated due process rules by exercising Engelhard's letters of guarantee, totaling approximately $20 million, and withholding additional refunds from the company amounting to an additional $10 million.

In accordance with their "standard practice," the Peruvian authorities appealed the Constitutional Court ruling. On May 28, 2004, the Fifth Civil Chamber of the Superior Court was assigned to decide the appeal. According to Peruvian law, Superior Court has twenty business days to render its decision, thereby establishing June 25, 2004 as the deadline. To date, not only has the Superior Court failed to rule, it has not even scheduled oral arguments in the case. The negative impact on hurdle rates for foreign investment and barriers to local capital formation logically follow from these arbitrary applications of regulatory rules.

Red Tape Hurts Mining Profits for South Africa

Thanks to booming commodity prices, the world's biggest mining companies had a spectacular year in 2005, with investment increasing by about 30 percent and profits by almost 60 percent. Despite such a strong year, South Africa's mining profits declined: investment declined by almost a third in 2004 and 2005 and profits by 12 percent. According to a survey carried out by the South African Chamber of Mines, red tape and regulatory uncertainty were partly to blame. They have cost the sector $0.7 billion to $1.4 billion a year in lost investment.[16]

In 2004, mineral rights were transferred from private to state hands and firms had to establish labor and social reforms to convert their existing licensees. Some of the big producers were granted new licensees for existing mines, but many others are still waiting. The vague rules that regulate the industry, some local lawyers argue, do not include measurable, objective targets for labor and social reforms and therefore cause the delays. A survey by the Fraser Institute, a Canadian research body, ranked countries by their governments' mining policies. South Africa came thirty-seventh out of sixty-four. Chile, where mining licenses are awarded by the courts based on clear criteria, ranked fourth.[17] Regulatory opacity emerged through the arbitrary granting of new licenses without application of any systematic and consistent rules. Politically mediated decisions enabling conversion from private to state ownership, appointment of management, and other nonbusiness interventions became common in those low-ranking countries. Licensing procedures, unless mediated by clear and consistent rules, are subject to political allocation.

Anticompetitive Regulatory Practices: The Case of Korean Chaebols

Instead of promoting competition and growth, certain regulations can often have the opposite effect. South Korea provides a useful lesson in this regard. The driving force behind Korean economic policy is the *chaebol*, a uniquely Korean business organization. The chaebols are large, diversified, family-run companies with extensive networks of subsidiaries and deep political connections.[18] Political favor is especially important to the chaebol, which has traditionally intervened extensively in government. The "Five-Year Plans," initiated in 1962, are a case in point. These plans sought to reorganize the nation's productive factors via regulation and reduce competition among South Korean firms in order to give global firms more power and leverage in the market [19]

The third Five-Year Plan was likely the most influential; it called for the development of South Korea's heavy manufacturing and chemical industries. The government encouraged the domestication of these industries via import regulations in order to promote national self-sufficiency.[20] However, the development of heavy industry under the third Five-Year Plan led to a concentration of wealth within the chaebol-owning families and the emergence of a dominant chaebol, crowding out competing firms well into the 1980s. This emphasis on heavy industry, and the resulting dominance of a small cadre of chaebols, led to the precipitous fall of the South Korean economy in the late 1990s.

But South Korea made changes and today its economy is growing, leading us to classify it as an "Edge" nation—a country where labor costs are higher and populations are smaller than India or China, for example, but transparency is much higher. Although the chaebols still maintain a great deal of control over the economy, they are no longer sacrosanct. They have been allowed to fail at times, and when they've erred prosecution has ensued. In fact, South Korean prosecutors are now serious when it comes to holding the chaebols accountable, and the country's overall transparency has increased as a result. Beginning in the late '90s, government prosecutors began investigating wrongdoings at the chaebols, earnestly sending senior chaebol officials to jail on corruption charges. More recently, prosecutors found evidence that the chairman and chief executive of Hyundai, one of South Korea's top automakers, had created a multimillion dollar slush fund. State prosecutors went so far as to detain him on March 27, 2006 while continuing their investigation. In February 2007, the chairman, a grandson of the automaker's founder, was sentenced to three years in jail.

Corporate Governance: Cases from the European Union

The volatility in emerging and established capital markets over the past few years reflects a growing recognition of the importance of institutional and market-based mechanisms that govern corporations. Corporate governance—an important opacity factor—reflects the economic dimension of governance in civil society and the capacity for firms and individuals to freely engage in productive activities and thereby create economic opportunities. The Asian Crisis and the Russian Crisis, the charges of crony capitalism that have rocked emerging markets, and the corporate scandals of the past few years in the United States have created common themes of improving transparency and accountability that emerge in debates about appropriate business and public policies.

In a broad sense, corporate governance is simply a way to deal with the principal-agent problem. Principals are shareholders, while agents are management and other intermediaries. Through checks and balances, corporate governance aligns the objectives of agents with those of the principals. This process increases the likelihood that the suppliers of finance to corporations will receive the expected return on their investment.

To the extent that the European Union's (EU) current corporate governance remains deficient, there is an opportunity for accession countries to rapidly improve their governance by adopting best practices from countries with higher governance rankings (for example, the United States, Singapore, and the United Kingdom) and, in fact, bypass countries like France and Germany in the quality of their governance. Investors are increasingly concerned about governance, as evidenced by a McKinsey poll suggesting that 56 percent of investors in Western Europe, 57 percent in North America, and 85 percent in Eastern Europe consider corporate governance to be equally as important as financial fundamentals, which emphasizes the importance of corporate governance reforms in accession countries.[21]

The Czech Republic. In pursuing liberalization policies more aggressively than some of its neighbors, the Czech Republic was an early reformer amongst the transition countries. However, its rapid privatization program, which made use of a voucher system whereby citizens were granted points to bid on stocks of privatized firms, resulted in highly concentrated ownership and corporate governance abuses. As in Russia, voucher-led privatization resulted in insiders making negative net present value investments and thereby transferring value from the overall firm to themselves. Concentrated ownership combined with a culture of regulatory forbearance and weak supervision has led to weak corporate governance in the Czech Republic.

The Czech Republic recently took steps toward improving governance, with many of these improvements spurred on by the country's application for EU membership. The legal responsibilities of insiders have been defined, a new fairly unrestricted mergers and acquisition regime has been instituted, and accounting standards have been strengthened. Publicly listed firms are now more in accordance with International Accounting Standards, as are the Czech Republic's standards for disclosure by listed companies. In addition to the accounting reforms, shareholder rights have been improved.

But creditor rights remain weak despite the amendments to the Bankruptcy Law that were introduced in 2000.

Hungary. Reforms to Hungary's corporate governance have been motivated in large part by its accession to the EU. Hungary's accounting practices are of relatively high quality and foreign firms operating in Hungary and Hungarian cross-national firms are required to meet International Accounting Standards. Shareholder rights are also fairly well established, with shareholders being allowed to institute civil actions against management and directors.

Hungary also has a liberal takeover regime with merger and acquisition activity reasonably unrestricted, which provides an important discipline to management. A key weakness in Hungarian corporate governance, however, is creditor rights. The development of a corporate bond market is hampered by the lack of firm legal foundations for secured debt. Secured creditors are not ranked first in the distribution of the assets of a bankrupt firm in Hungary.

Poland. Poland has adopted a more gradualist approach to market reforms. Nonetheless, it has made sufficient progress toward liberalization to conclude negotiations for accession to the EU. Shareholder rights are fairly well developed, with the Commercial Code setting out the fundamental rights of shareholders, including the right to vote at general meetings, preemptive rights, and the right to vote on merger proposals, debt issuance, and amendments of the company's articles of association.

Accounting standards remain weak in Poland, however, as companies listed on the Warsaw Stock Exchange are not required to meet International Accounting Standards. Instead, they are only required to meet the standards of Polish Generally Accepted Accounting Principles (GAAP). Yet, in practice, firms often exceed the modest listing requirements with respect to accounting and disclosure. Another weakness in Polish corporate governance lies in its lack of an efficient market for corporate control. Merger and acquisition activity has not been liberalized in Poland and there are no clear and disclosed rules or procedures for takeovers, resulting in a situation where managers are able to shield themselves from accountability.

Dealing Strategically with Regulatory Opacity

A country's regulatory framework can become a source of competitive advantage in attracting both direct and portfolio investments and increasing entrepreneurial business formation. The regulatory opacity score indicates how far along a country is in using its regulatory framework as an advantage in global competition for capital resources and business activity. Alternately, it shows how hobbled businesses are by regulatory chokeholds on economic activity. The existence and proliferation of governance regulations and institutional environments conducive to investment and investors are important. They limit a regulator's margins for arbitrary and corrupt intervention into competitive business processes. Regulations that reflect a high quality of rights by all economic players and don't restrict mobility and change are characteristic of institutional environments that produce faster and more equitable growth.

In short, regulatory opacity reduces growth. Better and more transparent regulatory institutions mitigate and even eliminate adverse impacts of regulation and enable them to be used for their explicit objectives of worker safety, civil security, or environmental standards, not anticompetitive, corrupt, or interest-driven goals. Streamlining regulations and increasing their openness, transparency, and ability to empower, rather than entrench, economic actors will limit the adverse impacts of misguided regulation upon macroeconomic performance.

Chapter Seven

Applications of CLEAR
for Business Success

CONSIDER THE CASE of Israel, a beleaguered and sometimes beleaguering nation in the middle of one of the
most strife ridden neighborhoods in the world. It is a country many
people know well from the news and personal visits. From the traditional way in which risk is viewed, Israel should be a place to avoid.
Its neighbors are often aggressive, there are claims and counterclaims
about its borders and threats and counterthreats regarding how those
claims will be settled. Every once in a while, a bomb explodes and,
periodically, Israel is engaged in wars with its neighbors. It is a nation
of seven million surrounded by six hundred million people residing
in countries whose sentiments toward Israel are more than a little
hostile.[1] And yet, Israel has a score of 34 on the Opacity Index, has
been growing at about 5 percent a year, and its stock market has

soared. It is considered a very attractive place for electronic, high-tech, and bio-tech investments. Intel, Microsoft, Motorola, HP, and many other firms have significant outposts in Israel. Its venture capital industry thrives and, next to the United States, has the second largest number of companies listed on NASDAQ in the world.

For all these reasons, Israel, along with Thailand, Malaysia, Korea, and Taiwan, is designated as one of our Edge nations, where the cost of doing business is subject to very few hidden costs. In Israel and the other Edge nations, what you see is pretty close to what you get. However, Edge nations are not the same as the top-scoring nations. Edge nations have opacity gaps, such as Malaysia's relatively poor record with respect to protecting patent rights, but their transparency in other arenas easily outweighs the risks of these gaps.

Or take the case of China, which scores poorly on our Opacity Index. By any objective standards, China is a corrupt, one-party state with Army and Party members often wanting a piece of the action. China's legal system is inadequate and foreign law firms are limited in how much they can do for their clients; at best, they can only assist Chinese law firms in looking after their client's affairs. Labor laws are lax, property rights are still in the process of being defined, and imminent domain does not require much in the way of court orders. If the government or a developer wants your land, the decision as to whether they get it is made behind closed doors. And when it comes to intellectual assets and trademarks, China has a history of piracy.

In addition, China's accounting is opaque and its corporate governance standards are still being set. The country has deep divisions between its rich and poor, with many economic and political demonstrations taking place each year, mostly in smaller cities. Shanghai and Beijing may look calm, but Huaxi and Shenyou are not. According to some estimates—though we cannot attest to their reliability—China was home to seventy-four thousand riots of one kind or another in 2005, with hundreds of people killed.[2] And, as if that were not enough, China's banks are fragile, despite plans to fix them.

Yet each year $54 billion makes its way from the rest of the world to China to invest in its future. At a growth rate of around 10 percent a year, China is doing very well in spite of its problems.

Though Israel and China are very different countries in scale and opportunity, they have both have important attributes that global businesses require. Israel has a highly trained, highly disciplined scientific and technological workforce with deep expertise in electronics, software, the biological sciences, informatics, and defense. Major high-tech and bio-tech companies with operations in Israel put up with that country's day-to-day problems in order to take advantage of its special areas of competence.

When it comes to China, the size of its market and the low level of its wages are powerful allures for business. In addition, China offers a dedicated workforce that is developing its skills rapidly. In the case of Israel and China—and many other countries—there are strategies for dealing with risks in order to take advantage of each country's strengths.

CLEAR Offers Firsthand Data

When attempting to gain a risk perspective on a country, the last place to look is the news—an admission we make with some sadness, given that one of us was once a journalist on the staff of the *New York Times*. Even so, in the United States in particular, international news reports are often better at misinforming than they are at educating business leaders. Print and electronic media too often focus on the big, political stories, missing altogether issues that are relevant to businesses. The news media is fascinated by high-impact, low-frequency risks, and rarely covers low-impact, high-frequency events. Stories about corruption or failing legal systems sometimes make it into Britain's *Financial Times*, but given their frequency and ubiquitous nature, they do not get their due.

In Edge nation Israel, the "if it bleeds, it leads" dictum still prevails when it comes to the news. Rockets falling and suicide bombers are good camera fodder, even if their real impact is small. We are not suggesting that when tragedy strikes it should not be covered, only that the camera alters the scene. In Israel, on-air correspondents wear flak jackets and khakis more often (it seems) as costumes for the camera than from need. Frequently, when the cameras roll, they are the only ones wearing that garb.

News cameras compress events that are historical, national, and dispersed into a single pinpoint on the screen, so that a problem in a single spot becomes generalized into what we think is the condition of an entire area. While far from problem-free, Israel is hardly the place portrayed on television. If it were otherwise, few big companies would be able to operate there, let alone insure those operations.

News from BRIC nation China is something of the opposite. Though there are many political demonstrations a year, as noted, the camera rarely focuses on them.[3] News from (and in) China is controlled. Unlike Israel, where journalists are quite free to move around and shoot video more or less where they want, they are strongly censored in China. Rather than loosening up on the controls, in China they are becoming tighter. In 2006, the Xinhua News Agency, a government-controlled entity, was given extensive leeway to dictate what foreign news agencies could report, taking on the role of a quasi censor.[4]

In Israel, we would argue, problems involving violence, in particular, are overreported. In China, on the other hand, too few of its problems—including its violent and political ones—make it into the news. For these reasons we advocate a brogues-on-the-ground approach to global business. Executives must do more than read a few reports, followed by a meet-and-greet fly-in to visit their business counterparts. They must also get a feel for the context in which business operates in the country they are considering for a location. No joint ventures or sizeable investments should be made without this knowledge and experience, unless the stakes are very low or they can be easily reversed. It's difficult to really get to know a country's ins and outs in less than a year of time, and without several prolonged visits. Each country has its nuances and many of them are easy to miss.

In the mid-1980s, for example, one of us was a frequent visitor to Sri Lanka. On paper the statistics for that island nation looked good. Though Sri Lanka was a low-wage country, average lifespan was equal to countries in the West, literacy was nearly 100 percent, income was distributed equally, and quality food and water were plentiful. Back then, companies began investing in Sri Lanka to take advantage of its inexpensive but well-educated work force. The first investments into Sri Lanka were in the tourism and garment sectors, followed by electronics assembly.[5]

But clues to an impending civil war were everywhere. At formal dinners hosted by Buddhist Sinhalese, vegetarian Hindu Tamils were often served inedible fare. And at coconut and fruit stands throughout the country a tragic situation was observed. In different parts of the country there were numerous occasions when blind and scarred fruit sellers were observed. When queried as to the reason for their disfigurement, the answer was always the same: acid was thrown in their faces. Some of this was attributed to jealousy, but most to friction between Sinhalese and Tamils. Though the official statistics indicated Sri Lanka was calm, reality showed something else: a sizeable number of unreported violent incidents. Sri Lanka had a dark side.

It is surprising how many people invest in a country without getting to know it first. And while sometimes this is not preventable, as when company "A" acquires company "B" and finds itself with assets in a country its executives can't find on the map, it is usually an avoidable situation. From our experience, site visits are important. But site visits combined with knowing what to look for is vital. The Opacity Index and its CLEAR scores provide an ideal framework for such an assessment. If a country scores poorly with regard to corruption, then a site visit must include research on-the-ground focused on that specific factor. Though delicate, the topic must also be broached with other foreign companies operating in the target country. Is corruption as bad as our Index scores it? How is it dealt with? Whose hands are out? Do things really get done once a bribe is given, or does it simply mean that once one person receives a "facilitation payment," another person enters the line? Can utilizing local partners solve the problem?

By using CLEAR as a map for each fact-finding visit, companies can gather enough information to plan strategies that will help them succeed. Simply flying in to visit with a potential partner or see the investment in person is never enough. Businesses need to view countries through a CLEAR lens.

CLEAR Allows Business to Bet on the Future

As researchers and experienced businesspeople, we believe strongly in the predictive power of capital markets. To us, markets are more than places where financial products are traded: they are aggregators of opinion. Markets cannot move up or down unless there is some uniformity of opinion about a country's prospects for the future within an extremely important group: the people who deploy capital. If these individuals agree that country "A" is a place where their money will be safe in the future, the markets rise. If fears about the future overwhelm them, the markets fall. Volatile, sideways markets indicate that people with capital just don't agree about a country's prospects. In our view, markets can be early or late, but they are almost never wrong. Just as surveys that measure various types of confidence can show which way a market is likely to move, the markets themselves are indicators of the level of confidence investors have in a country's future.

For years, the emerging markets of the world were strapped for capital. People of means who lived in these developing countries preferred putting their money to work in New York, London, Miami, Hong Kong, Singapore, and Switzerland, rather than at home. International investors eschewed Mexico City, Tel Aviv, Istanbul, Moscow, Riyadh, Johannesburg, and many other places in favor of countries that were more developed and more highly regulated.

But conditions change, as the Opacity Index shows. While the media may dispute it, and national leaders may disagree, in the wake of the Iraq War, and the subsequent run up in oil prices, the capital markets of the Middle East (Arab countries and Israel) soared. As shown in figure 7-1,[6] in the period after 2003, Egypt, a country that does not have much oil, was the world's best performing stock market. Egypt's stellar performance was closely followed by excellent performances by almost every other market in the region.

One could argue that the markets in these countries performed well because oil prices more than doubled during that period. But unlike periods in the past when oil prices rose, this time a great deal

FIGURE 7-1

Rising Middle East markets

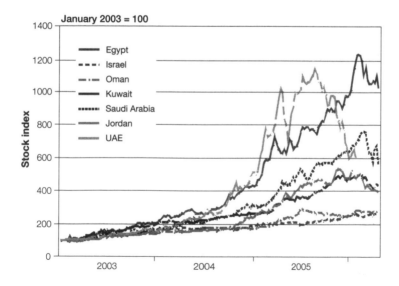

Source: Zawya.com, Milken Institute Global Conference, 2006.

of that money stayed at home or in the region. In addition, savvy investors in the United States, Japan, and Europe invested in those markets too.

If we accept the view that markets measure the level of agreement investors have about the future of a particular country, then rising markets in the Middle East are a very good indicator of what's to come. If people are placing big bets on the future of their countries and their regions, it is safe to say that this area's prospects have improved from the period in which the region's capital would have been exported to London, Zurich, or New York. For this reason, we strongly advocate examining how a country's capital markets are faring before investing there.

CLEAR and Access to Capital

If the capital markets measure confidence in the future on a macro level, then access to entrepreneurial capital measures two other important aspects of risk. First, it measures the strength of a country's financial institutions and their ability to move money where it is needed most: into the projects of entrepreneurs. Second, it measures whether there is an entrepreneurial class of people who are making *personal* bets on the future. Access to capital means someone, in some part of a country, is mortgaging his house or going to a bank or cooperative and borrowing money to build a business. By doing so, they are putting their own personal assets at risk.

The Milken Institute's Capital Access Index measures access to capital in countries around the world. As shown in table 7-1, this index can be used as an indicator of individual confidence in the future, and a yardstick by which to measure how that confidence changes from year to year. If the capital markets present the macro perspective, access to capital paints a picture of a country from the micro point of view. What is that picture? Simply this: if you invest in a country, will your partners, suppliers, customers, and fellow

TABLE 7-1

Milken Institute Capital Access Index

Country	CAI 2006	Rank 2006	Rank 2005
Hong Kong SAR	8.07	1	2
Singapore	8.00	2	3
United Kingdom	7.79	3	1
Canada	7.61	4	10
United States	7.59	5	4
Australia	7.55	6	7
Switzerland	7.52	7	12
Netherlands	7.50	8	13
Ireland	7.46	9	10
Sweden	7.35	10	5
Malaysia	7.12	12	16
Finland	7.09	13	9
Denmark	6.99	14	6
Germany	6.92	15	15
Japan	6.88	16	19
Thailand	6.61	19	30
South Korea	6.58	20	23
Austria	6.53	21	22
Chile	6.45	22	18
France	6.44	23	20
Spain	6.42	24	17
Israel	6.39	25	27
Portugal	6.37	26	26
Belgium	6.05	29	28
Saudi Arabia	6.00	30	33
Hungary	5.94	31	36
South Africa	5.81	32	24
Lebanon	5.78	33	48
Taiwan, China	5.76	34	25
Italy	5.63	36	31
Poland	5.54	38	45
Czech Republic	5.34	39	32
Greece	5.25	42	29
Mexico	5.24	43	43
India	5.18	46	53
China	5.15	47	38
Colombia	5.03	49	50
Brazil	4.95	50	40
Russia	4.79	53	51
Turkey	4.74	54	60
Philippines	4.67	56	58
MEAN	4.64	–	–
Argentina	4.57	57	66
Indonesia	4.34	63	57
Pakistan	4.23	65	74
Venezuela	3.70	79	80
Egypt	3.60	82	92
Nigeria	3.60	82	94
Ecuador	3.49	87	89

Source: Milken Institute, 2006.

Note: The mean CAI 2006 value is 4.64.

investors have sufficient capital to support you? We believe this is an important question to ask.

But even more so, knowing whether individuals in a country have access to capital—and comparing one country to another—shows whether or not people have a stake in a country's future. In places where capital is available and entrepreneurship thrives, there is less likelihood of instability since the populace as a whole has something to lose. We believe economic democracy, which requires access to capital as a full measure of economic participation, is as important as political democracy. It indicates the degree to which people have control over their fates and their futures.

CLEAR and Patent Protection

Companies that depend upon intellectual capital are especially vulnerable in high-opacity countries with lax legal protections. As discussed previously in an example about China, pharmaceutical firms are perhaps hardest hit in this regard. Pharmaceutical companies in India, China, and Malaysia copy drugs that are still under patent protection and sell them in their home markets at discounts, to the applause of activists around the world. But when the American, European, or Japanese pharmaceutical company protests, it is portrayed as heartless—a company whose sole aim is profits and whose business model is based on predatory practices and the exploitation of poor, sick people in the third world. Never mind that the Indian company that sells its products to the poor is selling "knock-offs" at a profit. And never mind that consumers in the West and Japan are forced to shoulder more of the burden for research since pharmaceutical companies are unable to recoup their investment outside of their home countries.

Rather than figuring out defensive strategies, companies that are aware of their CLEAR factor risks in each of their markets can anticipate where things are likely to go wrong and can take a proactive approach. If they know that piracy of foreign patents and processes won't be punished, they can joint-venture with local firms, acquire a local firm, or enter into master contracts in one country (Singapore, for example) even if they are selling into another (China). What they cannot do, however, is to wait and hope for the best.

Using CLEAR to Promote Global Competition

One of our aims in conducting and promoting our research has been to create awareness among policymakers that opacity is a drag on growth. Another aim has been to create a higher level of awareness among businesses about which threats matter most. With respect to countries, we have only just begun. Mexico has put our Opacity Index on its governmental Web sites in the hope that it will convince citizens at every level to become more open. Mexico understands that, while it has lost foreign direct investment to China and India, it can gain some of that investment back if it cleans up its act. Opacity adds a layer of hidden costs that make cheap labor not quite as cheap. We hope our index will promote some healthy competition among countries so that they will vie with one another to become more transparent. With businesses, our aim is raise awareness and improve decision making, not point fingers. We would like to help companies take prudent risks.

The world in which we live is far from safe. But the real threats to a company's future are too often overlooked. Political shifts happen and it is unlikely that we will ever be free of war. But corruption and the quixotic imposition of rules—or the lack of them altogether—can cost companies much more than these low-frequency phenomena. It is our hope that companies apply this research to make better decisions. It is also our hope that they use the CLEAR factors and our measurements of those factors as a road map, pointing them toward better and more profitable futures.

Chapter Eight

Country Risk

I N THIS CHAPTER we look more closely at a selection of
countries with Opacity Index ratings considerably above
or below the average for their income group. We also look at the case
history of a number of countries that score in the mainstream for their
income group but possess economies—and often, problems—of great
interest. We respond here to the simplest and most relevant of questions: what facts "on the ground" in these countries justify their ratings? The discussions are not survey-based; they are our views after
studying the data and each country's rules and regulations.

Opacity Profiles

In this section, we discuss how specific countries have created or
maintained their edge in global competition, focusing our attention
on various dimensions of their Opacity scores. As countries grapple
with their systems of economic and business information to disclose

or obscure their performance, much can be learned from the processes and outcomes of their efforts.

Ireland: A Robust, Carefully Managed Economy

With a population of some 3.8 million and a famously robust economy, Ireland offers a model in many respects to other national economies of its size and greater (see table 8-1). Thirty years ago, Ireland was a third world country, viewed not much differently than Paraguay or Malawi. Today, Ireland is one of the world's wealthiest countries. Its economy has grown nearly five-fold since 1973. It boasts one of the world's highest levels of GDP per capita, some twenty percent above the European average, while thirty years ago it was 35 percent poorer than the average.

Within the World Bank high-income group of countries, Ireland earned an outstanding overall Opacity Index rating. A country's financial system size reflects the level of stock market capitalization, bonds outstanding, and bank assets. Based on its Gross National Income per capita, every economy is classified as low income, middle income (subdivided into lower middle and upper middle), or high income. The interaction of financial development and economic growth in income are well-demonstrated in the case of Ireland.

With regard to corruption, public tribunals in recent years investigating alleged corruption in some areas of businesses and polit-

TABLE 8-1

Ireland

C	L	E	A	R	Opacity score	World Bank income group	GDP per capita	Financial system size
34	18	26	37	10	25	High	$48,604	7.3

ical life have improved the business climate. The Office of the Director of Corporate Enforcement (ODCE) was recently established, and the work of the Criminal Assets Bureau (CAB) has earned international respect. The Irish legal system retains its reputation for integrity and independence. Modernization of court services has been successfully pursued in recent years. There is a standing Law Reform Commission and a standing Company Law Review Group.

On the economic front, Ireland's success over the past number of years has been well documented, with a GDP for 2005 of 5.5 percent and 5.8 percent for 2006. A number of drivers contribute to this success, including an ever-stronger emphasis on training and education; a successful foreign direct investment (FDI) strategy since the 1960s; a favorable fiscal regime for corporations; a series of Partnership Agreements between government, the trade unions, and employers, which stipulate such cost drivers as national wage agreements; and EU support for a variety of initiatives that have improved the efficiency of doing business in Ireland.

Ireland has marched forward with respect to accounting and corporate governance. In mid-February 2002, the Tánaiste and Minister for Enterprise, Trade, and Employment, Mary Harney, announced that she would introduce new legislation governing the auditing and accounting profession.[1] Ms. Harney affirmed that "new requirements will ensure transparency in the relationship between companies and their auditors." Irish law in application to accounting and corporate governance now reflects the relevant EU directives and regulations covering companies, banks, insurance institutions, and other types of entities. U.K. accounting standards, published by the Accounting Standards Board, are promulgated for use in Ireland by the Institute of Chartered Accountants of Ireland.[2]

As to regulatory affairs, in recent years a series of independent regulatory authorities have been established in such areas as electricity, gas, airports, and consumer affairs. There is a Competition

Authority backed by up-to-date legislation, and the Central Bank, which currently regulates the banking sector, has set up a new Irish Financial Services Regulatory Authority.

Overall, Ireland offers a record of sustained and wise support for an increasingly transparent and productive business climate. Ireland's economic growth model has been hailed as an example of development done right. Much attention has been paid to removing opacity barriers to growth.

Italy: More Trasparenza Needed

With a population of 58.5 million, Italy is estimated to be more opaque than many other high-income countries, specifically in the legal, enforcement, and regulatory dimensions (see table 8-2).

Italy's relatively poor opacity ranking reflects almost impossible to follow audit trails and governance rules that have proved scandelously inadequate and that inhibit foreign investment. "Syndication" rules in Italian accounting practice enable cross-participation by key financial institutions in corporate ownership. The result is embedded ownership relationships enabling groups to obtain controlling interests with relatively low equity investment.

With respect to legal opacity, The Bank of Italy and Consob (the Italian stock market regulator) are the primary enforcers of laws guar-

TABLE 8-2

Italy

C	L	E	A	R	Opacity score	World Bank income group	GDP per capita	Financial system size
49	34	47	62	25	44	High	$30,200	3.18

anteeing shareholders' rights. However, they are typically less vigor-
ous in pursuing violations than, for example, their U.S. counterparts,
and punishment for abuses often consists of rather modest fines.

Economic and fiscal policy remains somewhat dependent on
the use of one-off measures and budgetary devices to ensure compliance with the Growth and Stability Pact (GSP). Finance ministers
from the fifteen EU nations criticized Italy's plan to balance its budget,
stating that "Italy must transform its one-off measures into structural
reforms."

On the regulatory front, a tendency to regulate through highly
detailed legislation has created an extremely complex system marked,
in the opinion of some observers, by ambiguities, bureaucracy, rigid
procedures, and a high level of regulatory burden on business. Furthermore, the OECD has suggested that there may be an insufficiently transparent framework for central government enforcement
of the application of EU Directives at the regional and local levels.[3]
Regulatory reform is on its way. In 1999, Law 50 was passed, which
seeks to rationalize all existing regulations, review their quality, and
simplify their administration in an effort to implement current best
practices and bring Italy into line with its peers and competitors.

Byzantine rules of business in Italy have led to staggering scandals, such as the recent case of Telecom Italia, the privatized national
telephone network. Telecom Italia charges more than most telephone
networks in Europe but has managed to lose money and share value
yearly while increasing debt to forty billion Euros. When Telecom
Italia sought to sell its profitable mobile phone division it was revealed that earnings from profitable divisions had been diverted into
two outside companies ("empty boxes," or part of the accounting
syndicate) controlled by some of the owners. In short, stripping the
telecom of its profitable assets was conducted to pay off debts and
transfer assets behind the backs of other shareowners. Opacity made
this possible.[4]

Germany: Great, Despite Difficulties

With a population of 82 million and one of the world's most ad-mired and productive economies, Germany is nonetheless estimated to be relatively opaque within its income group (see table 8-3). Many observers would agree that German individual and corporate tax laws are among the most complicated in the world. This complexity, combined with the frequency with which the laws are changed, con-tributes to opacity. Strict yet highly changeable government policies and regulations have burdened businesses and have made the busi-ness environment in Germany relatively more opaque than in com-peting economies.

The situation is not, however, locked in place. Tax and other reforms are underway and the government of Angela Merkel is inclined to free up the labor markets. The trend toward easing taxa-tion in recent years is also a positive sign. Regulatory opacity is ex-pected to decline as the EU seeks increased harmonization. Overall, however, Germany's relatively high levels of opacity, given its size and importance in the world, has made German equity capital much more expensive than, say, either the United States or the United Kingdom. If you add opacity into the mix, a picture emerges of an underperforming Germany mired in its own sluggishness and back-room negotiations.

TABLE 8-3

Germany

C	L	E	A	R	Opacity score	World Bank income group	GDP per capita	Financial system size
23	14	30	37	32	27	High	$33,854	3.85

Finland: Clarity and Energy in the North

With a population of only 5.2 million and per-capita GDP that ranks eleventh worldwide, Finland is one of the most admired, vibrant, and well-managed economies in the world. It proved to be a leader across all CLEAR dimensions of the Opacity Index (see table 8-4).

The 2005 Corruption Perception Index, published by Transparency International, ranked Finland second in corruption among 159 countries.[5] Finland also has very low levels of black market activity, and the government is striving to root out the gray economy, the flow of goods outside of distribution channels authorized or approved by manufacturers and producers, by special task forces and taxation rules. Regarding the country's legal framework, the laws that protect intellectual and other property rights are strong and well enforced by a highly efficient legal and judicial system. On March 1, 2000, the new Finnish constitution, which applies to all residents of Finland, both citizens and noncitizens, came into force. (Finnish society is governed in accordance with fundamental rights that guarantee all residents the same treatment regardless of their status.)

Accounting requirements are in full accord with EU Directives and are overseen by the Accounting Board of the Ministry of Trade and Industry. Listed companies meeting certain criteria may apply

TABLE 8-4

Finland

C	L	E	A	R	Opacity score	World Bank income group	GDP per capita	Financial system size
3	11	24	37	9	17	High	$37,504	3.04

IAS or US GAAP in place of Finnish rules in their consolidated financial statements, so long as these comply with EU Directives.

In the regulatory arena, the Act on the Openness of Government Activities was passed in late 1999. This legislation, guaranteed by the Constitution, ensures the right of individuals to access official information in the public domain. Finnish authorities have an obligation to disclose relevant information on their activities.

The tax authority deliberately emphasizes service, and tax legislation has been developed to ensure transparent procedures and the rights of tax subjects.

Finland is a small community with a relatively large number of interest groups and associations that advocate transparency in various ways and fields. The consensus that emerged in Finland after a deep recession in the early 1990s led to structural reforms that enhance competition and transparency. Reforms focused on regulatory, product, and market competition that enabled firms to overcome the problems of sparse population and long distances to large markets.

Japan: Immense Capability, Immense Problems

With a population of 127.7 million and a firm ranking as the second-largest economy in the world after the United States, Japan has faced difficult economic problems for a decade and has yet to find and apply effective remedies. Its overall Opacity Index rating poses the surprising phenomenon of a country with one of the world's highest per-capita incomes and, within its income group, a relatively high level of opacity. The CLEAR components responsible for the rating are enforcement of regulations and economic policy and accounting (see table 8-5).

While the Bank of Japan is officially independent and is clearly charged with an anti-inflationary role, Japanese monetary policy has recently been quite unpredictable. In 1999, the Bank of Japan adopted a "zero interest rate policy" and then abandoned it in August 2000.[6]

TABLE 8-5

Japan

C	L	E	A	R	Opacity score	World Bank income group	GDP per capita	Financial system size
33	21	30	22	22	26	High	$35,757	5.57

This was followed by a "post–zero interest rate policy" from August 2000 to March 2001, where the overnight rate was kept between 25 and 15 basis points, and then by "quantitative easing" from March 2001 to September 2001. Throughout these three policy stages, the Bank of Japan targeted the overnight call rate.

The concept of this unprecedented monetary policy experiment, commonly referred to as quantitative easing, was to stimulate the nation's stagnant economy. Under this policy, the Bank of Japan increased its target for "current account balances" of commercial banks at the Bank of Japan far in excess of their required reserve levels. The objective of this was to reduce the already low overnight call rate (which is roughly equivalent to the Federal Reserve's monetary policy instrument, the federal funds rate) effectively to zero.

More recently, in 2005 to 2006, Japan's growth has resumed. However, there are questions as to whether Japan will be able to sustain its momentum.

Japanese corporate disclosure practices remain the focus of much investor concern and are typically perceived as inadequate, incomplete, and insufficiently comparable to international accounting standards. Auditors in the United States and the United Kingdom continue to append disclaimers and implicit warnings to English-language versions of Japanese financial statements, and ratings agencies follow similar practices when rating Japanese firms. Much attention has been given to disclosure at Japanese firms, in light of past problems of large, underwater, off–balance sheet derivatives positions and current problems of massive and growing bad and risky debts.

Change appears to be on its way. Japan has taken some encouraging steps toward improving its accounting practices. For example, it has introduced market value accounting for financial assets as well as cash flow statements, tax-effect accounting, and retirement-benefit accounting.

The United States: Shaken and Angered

With a population of nearly 300 million, the world's largest economy, and the global responsibilities of the world's only superpower, the United States has been thrown into turmoil in recent months by events in widely divergent zones. Most pertinent here is the collapse of Enron Corporation, the largest bankruptcy in U.S. history, which revealed serious shortcomings in both the structure and the application of GAAP to complex transactions. While Congress, with Sarbanes-Oxley (SarbOx) legislation, tightened regulations, many on the ground deem that legislation too much, too stringent, and too expensive. As a result, the U.S. capital markets have lost ground to London (see table 8-6).

Reliable information is essential for efficient markets. But as financial technologies have evolved, so too have the complexities of reporting, due at least in part, to SarbOx. Complex capital structures that have afforded huge benefits to both investors and entrepreneurs

TABLE 8-6

United States

C	L	E	A	R	Opacity score	World Bank income group	GDP per capita	Financial system size
25	20	28	20	10	21	High	$42,000	4.32

have often evolved faster than regulatory and accounting standards and enforcement. Investors, employees, and the general public are now demanding greater transparency. Enron has brought to the surface needs in the following areas, among others:

- *Off–balance sheet activities.* As risk management practices and markets increase, companies can use a number of structures and entities to off-load both assets and liabilities from their balance sheets. Leasing and securitization are powerful and useful mechanisms of financial management, but reporting in this area needs improvement.

- *Derivatives.* Volatility in the pricing of derivatives makes traditional valuation practices based on historical costs impractical. Mark-to-market accounting has developed in some areas, but when applied selectively has serious impacts upon capital adequacy reporting. Applications to hedging are particularly difficult and neither universally understood nor applied.

- *Intangible assets.* As an increasing proportion of corporate assets is concentrated in intellectual property, brands, and goodwill, the importance of unified and consistent valuation strategies increases. As the economy moves increasingly toward knowledge-intensive and service-based activities, creating usable metrics for communications to investors becomes essential. The lack of consistent standards has created numerous problems in the transparency of accounting and reporting for securities markets sensitive to such valuations.

- *Revenue recognition.* Treatment of profits and reserves for losses offer enormous opportunities for obfuscation in financial reporting. Leasing capacity, customer acquisition cost deferrals, and similar potential distortions in the timing of booking various transactions have caused problems in many dynamic new industries (for example, the Internet, telecommunications, and other technology sectors).

- *Employee share options.* As companies have attempted to align the interests of employees, managers, and investors, the utilization of stock options as part of compensation has increased. The self-regulatory bodies (for example, the Financial Accounting Standards Board) as well as the SEC have yet to define and enforce consistent standards concerning how to include these amounts in cost and profit calculations.

Mexico: Open for Business

With a population of 105.3 million and remarkable complexity and richness across every dimension of society and culture, Mexico is estimated by the Opacity Index to be managing its affairs creditably across the CLEAR dimensions (see table 8-7). This brief overview focuses on the oversight and development of accounting and reporting.

The IMCP (Mexican Public Accountants Institute) has worked intensively on a series of Standardization Bulletins in order to give a normative platform, coordinating with international standards and practices, to the ever more complex business and financial operations of corporations. The Mexican Stock Exchange Commission issued Bul-

TABLE 8-7

Mexico

C	L	E	A	R	Opacity score	World Bank income group	GDP per capita	Financial system size
58	61	38	33	25	43	Middle (upper)	$7,298	1.25

letin 11-33, requiring information from every listed enterprise, much like SEC requirements in the United States, so that investors have a fuller and deeper view.[7] Other organizations, such as the IMEF (Mexican Institute of Finance Executives), have been active promoters of more complete financial information beyond currently mandated requirements.

In the financial sector, the National Banking and Insurance Commission requires several rather complex reports, including information on internal controls, in addition to the auditor's opinion on financial statements. The issuance of internationally accepted accounting and reporting standards in specialized sectors such as banking, securities trading, and insurance has been accelerated due to foreign investment.

The institution responsible for many aspects of Mexico's dynamic accounting and reporting culture is the Consejo Mexicano para la Investigación y Desarrollo de Normas de Información Financiera (Mexican Board on Research and Development of Financial Information). The Board focuses on five core issues:

1. Promoting understanding in the government, financial institutions, business, and professional, teaching, and accounting associations of the importance of transparency, objectivity, and reliability of information

2. Creating a Research and Development Center (RDC) to carry out research and to monitor new issuances and disclosure standards concerning financial information

3. Helping to determine how the accounting profession, and the community of criteria issuers and users, can best support the public interest and promote economic development in Mexico

4. Bringing the accounting practices of private and public enterprises nationwide into conformity with standards on financial information accepted worldwide

5. Disseminating the results of research carried out by universities, the financial community, business organizations, the government sector, and the accounting profession

Argentina: Striving Against Chaos

With a population of 37.8 million and a wealth of assets, from a highly literate workforce to a diversified industrial base and rich agricultural resources, Argentina has nonetheless been one of the most troubled of the world's economies in recent years. While its overall Opacity Index rating is average for its income group, its relatively low scores in the dimension of economic policy and regulation point toward the critical difficulties now facing the country, not all of which are of its own making (see table 8-8).

The underlying competitive position of the Argentine economy has deteriorated rapidly in recent years. Its export industries, particularly agriculture, were hard hit as world food prices dropped. The strong dollar in the late 1990s and Brazil's devaluation in 1999 made it hard to compete with cheaper prices from other countries. The jobless rate is now reported to be on the order of 16 percent, and 23 percent of the population is officially categorized as impoverished. Bank loans, if available at all, are costly: a large company may pay 12 percent interest, a small one may be required to pay 20 to 30 percent. Longer-term capital is hard to find and Buenos Aires's Bolsa de

TABLE 8-8

Argentina

C	L	E	A	R	Opacity score	World Bank income group	GDP per capita	Financial system size
62	63	42	30	25	44	Middle (upper)	$4,799	1.06

Comercio (the national stock exchange) is inadequate as a source of capital. Few shares are quoted, fewer still are liquid. New issues are rare and few smaller companies qualify to be listed.

The country's immediate economic crisis stems in part from the government's Austerity Bill passed in July 2001, which was designed to be a remedy by requiring budget reductions to decrease deficits and enable restructuring of the country's external debt.[8] A "zero deficit" law, as outlined by this bill, was intended to end deficit spending and slash state salaries and some pensions by up to 13 percent. Limits were placed on the amount of monies that could be taken from bank accounts, including monthly limits on cash withdrawals and caps on offshore transfers. The impact of these measures has brought protesters into the streets.

In such a chaotic context, orderly measures such as the Opacity Index and CLEAR factors may seem beside the point. However, economists and political analysts familiar with Argentina often refer to failures and misfortunes in the areas of fiscal policy and currency regulation, and also to corruption, as causes of the current disaster. There is ultimately reason for optimism—Argentina is extraordinarily endowed with physical and intellectual resources. Prudent management and reform across the CLEAR factors will be part of the solution.

South Korea: Modernizing Rapidly After Crisis

With a population of 48.3 million and an economy that grew in 2001 by approximately 4 percent, South Korea has found its way past the severe financial crisis of 1997–1999 and is reshaping its business environment across the CLEAR dimensions in positive ways. Owing to reported weaknesses in the legal, accounting, and governance dimensions, its overall Opacity Index rating is relatively weak for its income group (see table 8-9).

In our view, the data gives insufficient recognition to reforms in accounting and governance, brought about largely in response to

TABLE 8-9

South Korea

C	L	E	A	R	Opacity score	World Bank income group	GDP per capita	Financial system size
50	35	26	30	36	35	Middle (upper)	$16,308	2.93

the collapse of the Daewoo Group in 1999. While the public and some political figures may continue to dwell on the problems that caused the collapse, they point out that regulators, the major accounting firms, and other key participants have made enormous progress toward greater transparency:

- The reliability of financial information in the capital market has been considerably improved. Most companies' financial statements and audit reports are closely reviewed and monitored by the regulatory authorities in South Korea, and results are publicly announced.

- A new, independent, and private-sector accounting standards–setting body, the Korea Accounting Standards Board (equivalent to the U.S. FASB), has developed a series of new and revised statements of financial accounting standards. The new standards provide guidelines for accounting for complex transactions such as those involving derivatives, in conformity with International Accounting Standards and US GAAP.

- The accounting profession is required to apply such accounting standards strictly, as part of a national effort to move beyond the Daewoo collapse and related events. Most listed companies in South Korea are keenly focused on strict adherence to the new accounting standards. In addition, all banks and financial institutions in South Korea are presently adopting the new accounting standards set forth by the KASB, and some major banks are even adopting US GAAP for some purposes.

- Corporate governance in South Korea has been significantly improved by introducing independent directors (primarily in large listed companies) and audit committees composed dominantly of independent directors.

- Shareholder activism is now common, and the protection of minority shareholder interests has improved.

Indonesia: Still Struggling for Stability

With a vast population of 219.2 million, Indonesia has been one of the world's troubled economies—and societies—for some years. That its Opacity Index rating is mainstream for its income group, despite low scores with respect to corruption and the legal framework, may point to underlying strengths that will reassert themselves, given the right encouragement (see table 8-10).

We will restrict our commentary here to the legal dimension of CLEAR. The poor reputation of Indonesia's legal system and perception that the situation is deteriorating has been subject to intense discussion and media coverage recently. In particular, there is growing public dissatisfaction with the lack of progress in bringing to justice

TABLE 8-10

Indonesia

C	L	E	A	R	Opacity score	World Bank income group	GDP per capita	Financial system size
70	52	83	22	50	56	Low	$1,289	1.01

the small minority of wealthy and powerful individuals who are believed to have profited illegally at the expense of the majority of the Indonesian people, whose standard of living continues to deteriorate in the wake of the 1997–1998 financial crisis. At the same time, there is increasing concern for the enforceability of contracts and lack of certainty over legal title. Both are problems that can only serve to reduce business confidence and foreign investment. Although in 1998 Indonesia introduced for the first time a bankruptcy law intended to improve the process by which debt and other contracts could be enforced, in practice there have been few if any successful cases under this law, and many view it as ineffective.

The country's problematic legal framework results from a number of factors, including outdated or conflicting laws that create uncertainty, poor law enforcement, and the commonly held view that widespread corruption in the court system renders legal rulings unreliable. The situation is further complicated by a process of regional decentralization that is taking place, and which has caused difficulties for businesses, such as mining companies now subject to new and sometimes inconsistent regional government regulation.

Opacity in Transition: Case Studies

In this section, we examine several countries that are actively engaged in utilizing dimensions of the CLEAR scores to create a competitive strategy for growth. The countries range from China, of one of the world's most important transition economies, to smaller countries, like New Zealand and Estonia, that seek to identify and develop their competitive position in the global economy. Though these smaller economies were not included in our original survey, we have had the opportunity to examine them as they have actively embraced opacity reduction as part of their strategy for economic growth.

Case Study: China

Not until 1978, when Vice Premier Deng Xiaoping led reforms to open China to foreign markets and steer the centrally planned economy toward being more market-based, did its financial institutions undergo transformation and rapid modernization. During the decade that followed, the government created a central bank (the PBOC, restructured) and the so-called Big Four commercial banks, and allowed the first foreign banks to begin operations in China.

In the 1990s, the government established two stock exchanges and the first publicly traded private bank, and enacted and amended a number of laws, including the Commercial Banking Law, which allowed banks to make their own management decisions, assume their own risks, and bear responsibility for their financial solvency. The state also established three policy development banks to take over state-policy loan functions from the Big Four, thus allowing them to operate on the basis of "market rules." Four asset-management corporations, created in 1999, assumed control over substantial amounts of nonperforming Big Four loans.

By the end of 2006, the Bank of China (BOC), China Construction Bank (CCB), and the Industrial and Commercial Bank of China (ICBC) had been sufficiently restructured to operate as joint-stock banks. (The dual listing of ICBC set a new record for IPOs, raising a total of $19 billion on Shanghai and Hong Kong stock exchanges.) Additional regulatory agencies were established to oversee the banking, securities, and insurance industries, leaving the central bank responsible for monetary policy. The government also deregulated interest rates to provide more market- and risk-driven pricing for loans and deposits. The aim of all these actions was to enable Chinese banks to compete internationally as the country complied with its commitments to the World Trade Organization (WTO) to open its domestic banking market to foreign firms by 2007.

Yet despite numerous reforms and improved performance in China's financial sector, some observers express concern that Chinese banks may be vulnerable to disruption in the coming years. Their concerns center around three issues:

1. Substantial growth in bank credit in recent years and the possibility of continued growth may once again lead to a nonperforming loan problem as newly made loans age.

2. Domestic financial institutions that are still relatively weak may suffer from increased competition as China opens its financial sector to foreign firms.

3. The U.S. trade deficit with China—amounting to $233 million in 2006, up from $202 in 2005—contributes to pressure on China to revalue its currency (this is in addition to the 2 percent revaluation that occurred in July 2005, when the RMB was allowed to float in a narrow band). If China's trade surplus triggers a rise in the value of the RMB, export growth may slow and, if domestic spending does not sufficiently increase, the nation's economy will suffer, with banks left holding increased amounts of nonperforming loans.

China's financial system shows how regulatory opacity can occur through the structure of regulatory policy. The central bank (PBOC), the bank regulator (China Banking Regulatory Commission, or CBRC), the securities regulator (China Securities Regulatory Commission, or CSRC) and the insurance regulator (China Insurance Regulatory Commission, or CIRC) all report directly to the cabinet-level State Council. This regulatory structure reflects a "silo approach" to regulation, with a separate regulator for each of the three different types of financial service firms. There are financial conglomerates in China, but as yet no specific laws or regulations regarding their formation or activities. They operate with the approval and under the auspices of the State Council.

It is clear that China, with total financial assets of $5.5 trillion, has a significantly smaller financial system than that of the United States, whose assets totaled $53.6 trillion in 2005. The system composition differs for both, as well. China has a bank-centered financial system, while the U.S. system is oriented toward capital markets. In the United States, banks account for 23 percent of total financial assets, while corporate bonds and stocks account for 66 percent. In China, banks account for nearly 69 percent of all financial assets; corporate bonds and stocks constitute about 20 percent of total assets. This means that firms in China depend mainly on bank loans for external financing. It also means that with relatively underdeveloped capital markets, bank deposits are the primary financial instruments available for savings. When China's banks are in trouble, the country's entire financial system is in trouble. Its underdeveloped capital markets are not equipped to provide alternative funding sources if banks curtail credit because of a weakened financial condition, much less manage risks associated with complex financial crises and subsequent resolution.

The different kinds of financial institutions in China also vary and are not clearly regulated. There are approximately thirty-five thousand financial institutions, but nearly 95 percent of these are rural credit cooperatives. However, the four state-owned commercial banks, or Big Four, account for slightly more than half of total assets and operate nationwide through elaborate branch networks. For this reason, the Big Four receive the greatest attention when one assesses the financial condition of the banking industry in China or, for that matter, the entire financial system. Furthermore, this is why reform and restructuring efforts in recent years have been directed mainly at these particular institutions. The joint-stock commercial banks have also received considerable attention because even though there are only twelve such institutions, they account for 16 percent of the total assets of all financial institutions. Sixteen institutions, in short, account for two-thirds of total assets. These banks not only receive the most attention from the regulatory authorities but also attract the most interest from foreign firms entering China. Detailed information on the different segments of China's financial industry reinforces the importance of the Big Four, both in terms of their share of total assets of all depository institutions and their share of loans and deposits. The size of the corporate bond market is also considerably smaller than noted above when one considers just corporate bonds issued by nonfinancial firms (only 4.4 percent of the current market).

Case Study: Estonia

With a small population of 1.4 million in a country roughly the size of Vermont and New Hampshire combined, Estonia is a member of the World Trade Organization and a candidate for accession to the European Union. It has a growing economy and sophisticated leadership in both government and business.

Estonia's remarkable achievements in decreasing opacity during its transition years within its income group can be explained by the cumulative effect of many factors. Estonia was able to start reforms early, as compared to many other transition countries—thorough reform of both the social order and business life started at the beginning of the 1990s. A strong framework of laws allowed reforms to succeed and avoided the confusion that can lead to entrenched corruption.

In the last decade, the country has been led mainly by right-wing coalitions with a clear market orientation. The drive to gain accession to the EU has helped to smooth the way toward unifying Estonia's legal environment with that of Western Europe. Business activity in Estonia has been supported by a relatively simple tax system, a uniform 26 percent income tax rate. Corporate income tax relief applicable to investment was introduced some years ago.

The Accounting Law, effective since 1995, corresponds by and large to IAS and has contributed to the transparency of the business environment. Unlike many transition countries where, for example, only listed companies are subject to annual audits, in Estonia the accounts of all entities operating as public limited companies must be audited.

Case Study: New Zealand

Another small country finding its place in the global economy is New Zealand.

With a population of 4.03 million and a robust economy, New Zealand has the potential to become the Finland of the Pacific— small in scale, but vigorously competitive in world markets. New Zealand has a proud record of being free from corruption. A number of factors contribute, including a democratically elected government, a strong judicial system that is independent of the executive, independent media, and public services that operate on the principles of probity and professional excellence.

Investors, the business community, and society at large have confidence that lawful contracts are upheld and enforced by New Zealand's robust legal system, developed on the basis of British law. There is comprehensive legislation dealing with investor rights, and rights are generally enforced through the courts with rights of appeal, in some cases, to the Privy Council in London.

A number of mechanisms ensure a high level of transparency surrounding economic policy and assist in creating a climate of "no surprises," which is regarded in New Zealand as essential for sustained business confidence. An annual statement at the commencement of each parliamentary term outlines the government's policy intentions at a strategic level. The Budget and Fiscal Economic Update, usually delivered in May or June each year, sets out detailed policies for the following year. The December Economic and Fiscal Update provides analysis of the previous year's activity and updates the budget.[9]

Fiscal policy must conform to the Fiscal Responsibility Act, which, as the name suggests, imposes obligations on government to pursue fiscally prudent policies. For some years now, fiscal policy under successive governments has been based on running operating surpluses, keeping net Crown debt below 20 percent of GDP, and keeping central government expenditure at approximately 35 percent of GDP.

Operating independently of the government, New Zealand's central bank, the Reserve Bank of New Zealand, is responsible for the formulation and implementation of monetary policy and prudential supervision. A Policy Targets Agreement is entered into between the Bank's Governor and the Treasurer. Currently, this Agreement requires the Bank to maintain inflation within a range of 0–3 percent.[10] New Zealand has had many years of low inflation.

New Zealand has a comprehensive set of financial reporting standards aimed at promoting transparency and good governance. The Accounting Standards Review Board is a Crown entity established to approve financial reporting standards to apply to entities reporting under the Financial Reporting Act 1993. The Institute of Chartered Accountants has taken the lead in submitting standards to the Board for approval. In general, the Institute has developed exposure drafts for standards based on the equivalent International Accounting Standard or Australian standard, whichever is more appropriate. Under the Financial Reporting Act, reporting entities are required to prepare financial statements that comply with generally accepted accounting practice. Auditing standards in New Zealand are in line with the standards generally recognized internationally.

Corporate governance is recognized in New Zealand as being an important contributor to corporate performance and lowering the cost of capital. New Zealand has an active Institute of Directors, which offers a wide range of courses and other support mechanisms aimed at instilling good corporate governance practices.

New Zealand's regulatory regime emphasizes creating a level playing field and removing barriers to competition. This applies across product, capital, and labor markets. The country's approach to regulation has been popularly referred to as "light handed"—meaning that in New Zealand the design of regulatory frameworks seeks to minimize compliance and wider economic costs.

Government support for free trade is reflected in a liberal regulatory regime for foreign investment. It also supports competition as a means of promoting economic growth and efficiency, and this is reflected in the framework for protecting consumer interests including, in particular, the Commerce Act and Fair Trading Act.

There is comprehensive legislation in place to protect investors' rights, principally the Companies Act, which provides the framework for the formation and governance of companies, and the Securities Act, which seeks to promote the efficiency and protect the integrity of capital markets.

Chapter Nine

Why Opacity Matters

TODAY'S GLOBALIZATION is a resumption of trends that preceded World War I. Indeed, many of the present debates about globalization and the problems of opacity echo concerns of that period. In examining globalization before World War I, a sobering picture emerges. Then, as now, opacity played a crucial role in destabilizing events that disrupted the twentieth century. The economy of the late nineteenth century was one of rapid globalization: capital and labor flowed and commodity trade boomed as transport costs dropped. The convergence of income, prices, and wages that occurred from 1850–1914 due to open trade and mass immigration came to a halt from 1914–1950 as deglobalization and autarky emerged as dominant economic and political trends. Opacity ruled and capital flows quickly faltered, triggering economic crises and political instability. Undeveloped capital markets, rule of law and regulation, enforcement, and obtuse business practices corrupted, both literally and operationally, economic operations with enormous political consequences. We would not want to go back to that future in the twenty-first century.

The two driving forces of globalization are technology and liberalization; both require and generate transparency. The natural barriers of time and space that separate national markets are collapsing at record speed as communication, information, and transportation technologies are transforming and integrating national economies. Nevertheless, opacity within these national markets creates friction in transitioning toward a global growth economy.

In examining product, labor, and capital markets, the degree of integration today can be overstated. Though the ratio of trade to output in product markets has increased sharply in most countries since World War II, it is not substantially higher in Western European countries than it was in 1914, and in Japan it is relatively less. Price convergence across countries is still elusive, and other indicators of product market integration still lag. Financial markets are also not fully integrated. Until recently, the index of capital controls was declining and net private capital flows by banks, foreign direct investment, and portfolio investment were increasing. In a strict test of capital market integration, real (inflation-adjusted) interest rates should converge; but real interest rates differ substantially still, even in our low-interest rate environment. Only 10 percent of domestic investment in emerging economies has been financed from abroad. Home biases remain strong.[1] Foreign direct investment relative to domestic GDP is smaller now than during the period before World War I. The net outflow of capital (that is, the current account surplus) for most developed countries is actually lower than before World War I. Today the average level of current account balances has not quite attained the magnitude common before World War I. Labor markets are considerably less integrated than at the turn of the century, despite integration of product and capital markets.

In short, gross capital flows may be very large, but net flows are actually smaller than those observed during the period of the gold standard. Trade flows are not significantly higher than they were prior to 1914, if measured against GDP, but are higher if measured against industrial production. While international investment flows commonly topped 3 percent of GDP before 1914, they slumped to less than half that level in the 1930s and only began to move upward after 1970.

An important lesson from the implosion of past globalization is that growing nation-state and intrastate inequality created a backlash against globalization. Significant distributional events caused a drift toward more restrictive policies: in trade, migration, and capital investment flows. The deglobalization implosion after 1914 was not independent of economic events. The retreat from free trade that culminated in rabid protectionism after World War I was manifested in protection of domestic agriculture from negative price shocks associated with globalization and trade-induced deterioration in the relative position of classes within Europe and the United States.[2]

Today, with enormous liquidity in global capital markets and with many global corporations and financial institutions overcapitalized, the investment challenges facing most businesses must be carefully weighed and measured before pulling the trigger on investment in portfolios, offshore projects, or business acquisitions. The flows of credit between developing and emerging-market economies has been transformed in recent years as developing country companies shifted from borrowers to large net lenders and partners of developed corporations. Low interest rates internationally imply too much saving relative to the amount people want to invest.

Overcoming this investment and growth gap for most countries is the key to unlocking international and regional prosperity. Global firms remain reluctant to invest, creating savings surpluses or "glut" (as Federal Reserve Board Chairman Ben Bernanke has called this condition), which leads to a pileup of foreign reserves and a primary concern to protect exports rather than encourage domestic investment and consumption. The weak appetite for investment explains low interest rates, but the rising imbalances in investment patterns can only be understood by examining the differences between countries' economic, legal, regulatory, and business practices and structures, and how business and public policymakers in those countries respond to needs for structural changes. This is precisely what the Opacity Index measures.

For the many countries without a savings glut, domestic savings are inadequate for fueling capital formation for economic growth and job creation. Portfolio capital flows are of increasing importance. Net portfolio flows represent a substantial and growing part of the impact of globalizing capital markets upon economic growth and development in both developed and emerging market countries. The share of foreign direct investment and portfolio equity in the financial mix of many developing countries has grown in recent years and needs to grow further to enhance political stability and economic growth. For example, equity flows amounting to over \$1.4 trillion globally accounted for 80 percent of total external financing to developing nations during 1999–2005, compared with just 60 percent from 1993–1998.[3] The debate about the policies that might encourage or discourage stabilizing portfolio flows versus those that might promote "hot money" destabilizing effects on both emerging and developed economies is key to financing global futures. Global Indexes (FTSE, S&P, and MSCI) represent important benchmarks and result in portfolio weightings by investors that can radically affect capital flows into countries and their economic futures. In the realm of offshore projects and direct investment, corporations understandably have found these projects to be more risky and less of a contribution to shareholder value. Because of these risks, companies can make serious errors. Given these higher risks, we have developed the Opacity Index as a mechanism to better estimate the extra premium in the discount rate adjustment that should be applied. As we have shown in this book, the Opacity Index provides a further filter to estimate everyday risks not captured by existing measures.

Regulatory frameworks, as the Opacity Index shows, have exacerbated problems of investment through both equity and credit channels of capital flows. For example, present bank regulation evaluates asset riskiness individually by using risk-based capital standards.[4] The Opacity Index, building upon insights of modern portfolio theory, offers a different view, namely that portfolio risk is not additive: the riskiness of a portfolio is an entirely different thing from the sum of the risks of the individual assets. Diversification lowers risks, but understanding where and how to diversify requires understanding the rule-based mechanisms of the market and how easily they are being applied to business practices. As we have stated earlier, current tools are inadequate to this task. Value at Risk (VaR) estimates the potential loss—with a degree of confidence—due to adverse events under normal business conditions over a given time period. It is not, however, concerned with unusual conditions—low-probability, but high-cost events that can wipe out an entire investment. The Opacity Index helps to understand the likelihood of normal events that can create unusual types of risk circumstances.

Ratings agencies, such as Moody's, have cautioned against reliance on a single indicator, such as VaR, which can be unfit or misleading. Assessing potential stress events should be part of management decision making and risk-appetite processes. Opacity risks set the stage for the $2 trillion that were lost in financial crises in recent years ($1 trillion in Japan, $600 billion in China, $200 billion in South Korea, and $120 billion in Thailand). What the Opacity Index has done is create a data reduction tool to continuously monitor financial reform and structural changes by collecting relevant information from verifiable sources. Using the information assembled, we have shown how a business decision maker can map indicators showing whether or not policies promote efficiency, safety, and soundness in investment processes. This also enables us to anticipate future shifts in opacity risks.

As we have laid out in chapter 2, the Opacity Index can be used to plan scenario investments for everything from portfolio to offshore projects to merger and acquisition decisions overseas. The Index can generate customized opacity scores weighted for specific risk exposure.

The tools provided by the Opacity Index provide a lens through which to understand and evaluate investment decisions. The linkages between opacity risks and investment rewards have enormous implications for global growth and prosperity. The economics underlying this process are simple. Growing securities markets, foreign direct investment through offshore projects, and business combinations affect labor markets through the supply side. Market capitalization and valuations combine two things that make assets a desirable investment: the current rate of profit and the price that investors will pay for those profits. When the market is highly and correctly valued (minus the distortions of opacity), assets are worth more than they cost, so additional fixed investment makes sense. Resultantly, a shift toward higher investment increases employment at any given level of aggregate demand. As recent Nobel Laureate Edmund Phelps showed, highly valued markets indicate that profits from investment have increased and/or that the market value of those profits increased, resulting in higher employment.[5]

Countries that have structured their markets to receive relatively large direct and portfolio capital inflows have seen a disproportionate growth in transaction volume, liquidity, market capitalization, and growth in bank loans to the private sector. The ratio of liquid financial assets to GDP will have a strong correlation with subsequent economic growth in the decades ahead. Domestic firms learn from foreign investment enterprises evidencing positive spillovers from foreign direct investment. The overall effect of diminishing market opacity is positive for countries that can take advantage of investment spillovers in export growth, domestic demand, and additionally triggered domestic investment.

The need for diminishing global opacity is especially keen for a majority of countries struggling to overcome centuries of income, wealth, and educational polarization and enter a period of growth. Capital access and investment denied is all too often translated into democracy and freedom deferred, accompanied by political instability that hobbles global development. Overcoming opacity has implications beyond a specific business investment decision. The key to global growth and stability is the ability of ordinary people to realize their hopes and dreams in their business, professional, and home lives. This, in turn, requires low and stable interest rates and an overall stable macroeconomic environment. The main barriers to achieving these goals derive from opacity—the lack of stable, hard currencies and credible central banks, the existence of illiquid and poorly or inappropriately regulated capital markets, the lack of well-functioning and adequately capitalized financial institutions, and the absence of rule-based business practices, accounting, and enforcement. To meet the long-term needs of global growth, the lessons of opacity should be learned and applied to investment decisions, creating incentives and benchmarks for change in national economies around the world.

Investment—direct, portfolio, and project—is key to change. Simply because a country exhibits opacity risk should not preclude investment within its borders. Opacity risk alone is not the enemy of business; the true enemy is the ignorance or inability to measure and assess it. Opacity risks clearly reduce investment attractiveness, but these risks must be measured against growth potential, competitive advantage, and global strategic goals. By understanding opacity, we hope we have shown how business investment decisions can be weighed and measured and ultimately become transformative as agents of change. Ultimately, knowledge of those risks will reduce those sources of uncertainty. Whether investing in a power plant, telecommunications, trade, merger, or acquisition, each case requires assessing opacity risk in the context of corporate strategy and the capital structures created for global investment.

Notes

Introduction

    1. Joel Kurtzman, Glenn Yago, and Triphon Phumiwasana, "The Global Costs of Opacity," *MIT Sloan Management Review* 46, no. 1 (2004): 38–44.

Chapter 1

    1. Jens Erik Gould, "Venezuela Disavows 1980s-Era Bonds," *New York Times*, March 7, 2007.

    2. *Sarbanes-Oxley Act of 2002,* HR 3763, 107th Congress (July 30, 2002).

    3. Joel Kurtzman, Glenn Yago, and Triphon Phumiwasana, "The Global Costs of Opacity," *MIT Sloan Management Review* 46, no. 1 (2004): 38–44.

    4. Evo Morales, "We Need Partners, Not Bosses," address to the United Nations, September 22, 2006.

    5. Jennifer L. McCoy and David J. Myers, eds., *The Unraveling of Representative Democracy in Venezuela* (Baltimore, MD: Johns Hopkins University Press, 2004).

    6. Larry Rohter, "A Leftist Surges in Brazil's Turbulent Presidential Election," *New York Times*, May 17, 2002.

    7. Aon Corporation, *Political & Economic Risk Map*, 2006. http://www.aon.com/about/publications/pdf/issues/2006_P&E_Risk_Map.pdf.

    8. Ibid.

    9. It sold them back to the public a decade later.

    10. "U.N. Report Reinforces Security Council Divisions," CNN.com, February 14, 2003, http://www.cnn.com/2003/US/02/14/sprj.irq.un/index.html.

    11. James R. Barth, Tong Li, Don McCarthy, Triphon Phumiwasana, and Glenn Yago, "The Economic Impacts of Global Terrorism: From Munich to Bali," working paper, Milken Institute, Santa Monica, CA, October 2006.

    12. Home Office, Foreign and Commonwealth Minister, Report on Drug Trafficking in Keny and its Effect on Britain, 2006.

    13. Daniel Kaufmann, "Myths and Realities of Governance and Corruption," World Bank, Washington, DC, 2003.

    14. U.S. Department of Justice, *Foreign Corrupt Practices Act of 1977*, 2000. 15 U.S.C.

Chapter 2

1. Dennis Nally, "PricewaterhouseCoopers' CEO Survey," Pricewaterhouse-Coopers, LLC, 2005.

2. Our first research attempt, conducted in 1999, was survey-based. In later attempts, we realized that we could conduct our research with more precision if we changed our methodology and relied instead on statistical data. Overall, we use as many as seventy sets of data per country to create our country rankings and figure out costs. The charts in this chapter are based on data collected between 2001 and 2005. Our approach to measuring opacity required us to look directly at both processes and behaviors. While the results of both types of assessment—survey and "bench research"—were similar, studying both processes and behaviors has given us a deeper level of insight into conditions on the ground. For example, when examining a country's legal system in our research, rather than talking exclusively to lawyers, we now look at basic statistics and actions as reported in accounting, regulatory, and legal procedures associated with CLEAR indicators. As a result, we actually compare the number of procedures it takes to get a case heard in court on a country-by-country basis. In addition, we look at whether creditors have rights and whether there are such things as legally identified property rights. In each of our CLEAR categories, we look at dozens of relevant indicators and blend them together into a picture of how smoothly or poorly a country's systems really work. Some of our research is binary: Do creditors have rights? Are banks required to have independent audits? Must firms account for financial assets at market value? Other items are simpler: How many days does it take to open a new business? Where does the country rank on various corruption indexes? Overall, we use as many as seventy sets of data per country to create our country rankings and figure out costs.

As a result, what we are measuring is no longer opinion but data. We are interested in understanding how much sand is in each country's gears because we know that each grain of sand adds to a company's cost. We also know that when a grain of sand is removed, a country's level of transparency is improved and its costs go down.

3. Financial repression is a combination of controls on international capital flows and restrictions on domestic interest rates. The result is an artificially low cost of domestic funding to governments, squeezing out the private sector from credit markets. The government revenue from financial repression is the difference between the foreign and the domestic cost of funds, times the domestic stock of government debt. Keynes was the first to recognize this process in demonstrating that in order for entrepreneurs to invest, they must obtain sufficient short-term finance during the period of producing the investment and be reasonably satisfied that they can eventually fund short-term obligations by a long-term issue on satisfactory conditions. For both aspects of this twofold nature of investment to occur, it made "no difference to the amount of 'finance' which has to be found by the markets as a whole, but only to the channel through which it reaches the entrepreneur." See Fred R. Glahe (ed.), *Keynes's The General Theory of Employment, Interest, and Money: A Concordance* (Savage, MD: Rowman & Littlefield, 1991).

4. Extending the decimal point for the Opacity Index scores, no country scored exactly 35.

5. The lack of comparable sovereign bonds at a point in time limits the use of individual sovereign bond rates as a proxy for the cost of capital. Using International Finance Statistics (IFS) country data, which follows the IFS data guidelines, may provide a useful approximation of the cost of capital. In this regard, Cyrill Monnet and Warren E. Weber, "Money and Interest Rates," *Federal Reserve Bank of Minneapolis Quarterly Review* 25/4 (Fall 2001) use IFS government bond yields in a recent study published in the *Federal Reserve Bank of Minneapolis Quarterly Review*

6. International Monetary Fund, *International Financial Statistics* (Washington, DC: International Monetary Fund, 2001).

7. Ibid.

8. James Barth, Tong Li, Sangeetha Malaiyandi, Donald McCarthy, Triphon Phumiwasana, and Glenn Yago, "Capital Access Index 2005: Best Markets for Entrepreneurial Finance," research report, Milken Institute, Santa Monica, CA, 2005.

9. In fact, variables relating to the size, liquidity, and degree of development of a country's capital markets are used, in part, to calculate its Capital Access Index score.

10. Geert Bekaert, Campbell R. Harvey, and Christian Lundblad, "Liquidity and Expected Returns: Lessons from Emerging Markets," working paper 11413, National Bureau of Economic Research, Cambridge, MA, 2005; Wolf Wagner, "Diversification at Financial Institutions and Systemic Crises," Tilburg University, Center for Economic Research, Discussion Paper 72, 2006.

11. In our research, seventeen countries are considered to be least opaque among the countries studied. They include the United Kingdom, Finland, Hong Kong, the United States, Denmark, Singapore, Chile, Belgium, and others, but not the entire list of "High Income" countries as so designated by the World Bank. For purposes of illustrating the economic cost of opacity, these seventeen countries are used as the benchmark.

12. The estimation is based on a simple linear transformation of a study in the 2001 Opacity Index. PricewaterhouseCoopers Endowment for the Study of Transparency and Sustainability (2001).

13. Michael E. Porter, Klaus Schwab, Xavier Sala-I-Martin, and Augusto Lopez-Claros, eds., *The Global Competitiveness Report 2003–2004* (New York: Palgrave Macmillan, 2005).

14. Although we have not included Jamaica formally in our study, we have analyzed its opacity components.

15. International Monetary Fund, 2005 World Economic Outlook Database (Washington, DC: International Monetary Fund, April 2005).

Chapter 3

1. "About Transparency International: What Is Corruption?" Transparency International, http://transparency.org/about_us.

2. Klaus Uhlenbruck, Peter Rodriguez, Jonathan Doh, and Lorraine Eden, *Global Corruption Report 2005* (Berlin: Transparency International, 2005).

3. Kat McGovern, "Ethnicity, Conflict and Peacebuilding: The Case of the Solomon Islands," International Relations and Asian Politics Department, Unpublished M.A. Thesis, University of Queensland (2003).

4. Shang-Jin Wei, "How Taxing Is Corruption on International Investors?" *Review of Economics and Statistics* 82, no. 1 (2000): 11; Axel Dreher, Christos Kotsogiannis, and Steven McCorriston, "Corruption Around the World: Evidence from a Structural Model," *Public Economics* 5, no. 2 (2004): 305–312.

5. Shang-Jin Wei, "Domestic Crony Capitalism and International Fickle Capital: Is There a Connection?" *International Finance* 4, no. 1 (2001): 15–45.

6. Paul Volcker, "The Management of the United Nations Oil-for-Food Programme: Volume III, Report of Investigation," September 7, 2005, http://www.iic-offp.org/documents/Sept05/Mgmt_V3.pdf.

7. Ibid.

8. "Experts Meet to Hone Guide to Financial Soundness Indicators," *IMF Survey* 31, no. 19 (2002): 328.

9. Patrick Honohan and Daniela Klingebiel, "Controlling the Fiscal Costs of Banking Crises" in "Managing the Real and Fiscal Effects of Banking Crises," eds. Daniela Klingebiel and Luc Laeven, discussion paper 428, World Bank, Washington, DC, 2002.

10. James. R. Barth, Dan Brumbaugh, Glenn Yago, and Lalita Rameesh, "The Role of Governments and Markets in International Banking Crises," *Financial Services: Public and Private Policy* 10 (1998): 36-62; J. R. Barth, Steven Caudill, and Glenn Yago, "Cross-Country Evidence on Banking Crises: Do Financial Structure and Bank Regulation Matter?" in *Bank Fragility and Regulation: Evidence from Different Countries*, ed. George Kaufman (Amsterdam: Elsevier, 2000), 3–23.

11. "Corruption Perceptions Index 2005," Transparency International, http://www.transparency.org/policy_research/surveys_indices/cpi/2005.

12. David T. Johnson, "Bureaucratic Corruption in Japan," working paper 76, Japan Policy Research Institute, Encinitas, CA, 2001; David T. Johnson, *The Japanese Way of Justice: Prosecuting Crime in Japan (Studies on Law and Social Control),* (New York: Oxford University Press, 2005).

13. Johnson, *The Japanese Way of Justice*; Daniel Kaufmann, "Myths and Realities of Governance and Corruption," World Bank, Washington, DC, 2003.

14. Johnson, "Bureaucratic Corruption in Japan."

15. Josephine Roque, January 16, 2007, "Former VW Boss Faces Corruption Case," http://www.allheadlinenews.com/articles/7006158409

16. "Germany: Auditors Detail VW Corruption in India and Czech Republic," CorpWatch, November 11, 2005, http://www.corpwatch.org/article.php?id=12772.

17. Ting Gong, "Forms and Characteristics of China's Corruption in the 1990s: Change with Continuity," *Communist and Post-Communist Studies* 30 (1997): 277–288.

18. Ibid.

19. Japan, Denmark, and the Netherlands were criticized for having signed on to the 1999 OECD anticorruption and antibribery conventions, while failing to prosecute any of their own citizens.

20. Kerin Hope and Theodor Troev, "Bulgaria: Corruption Is Still a Key Stumbling Block," *Financial Times Limited,* May 19, 2006.

21. Lydia Polgreen, "Nigeria: High-Level Bribery Scandal," *New York Times*, March 23, 2005.

22. Tom Ashby, "Nigerian Oil Security Raised Amid Rebel Threat," Reuters, September 28, 2004.

23. Peter T. Leeson and Russell S. Sobel, "The Impact of FEMA on U.S. Corruption: Implications for Policy," Mercatus Center, George Mason University, January 11, 2007, http://www.mercatus.org/repository/docLib/20070111_The_Impact _of_FEMA_on_US_Corruption.pdf.

24. Organization for Economic Co-operation and Development, "United Kingdom: Phase 2 Report on the Application of the Convention on Combating Bribery of Public Officials in International Business Transactions and the 1997 Recommendation on Combating Bribery in International Business Transactions," April 12, 2007, http://www.oecd.org/dataoecd/62/32/34599062.pdf.

Chapter 4

1. Jayne O'Donnell and Andrew Backover, "Ebbers' High-Risk Act Came Crashing Down on Him," *USA Today*, December 11, 2002.

2. U.S. Congress and U.S. Senate, *Sarbanes-Oxley Act of 2002,* publication no. 107-204, 116.

3. Alexei Barrionuevo, "The Enron Verdict: The Overview: Two Enron Chiefs Are Convicted in Fraud and Conspiracy Trial," *New York Times*, May 26, 2006.

4. Daniel Kaufmann, "Anti-Corruption within a Broader Developmental and Governance Perspective: Some Lessons from Empirics and Experience," statement by Head of the World Bank Delegation to the High Level Political Signing Conference for the United Nations Convention Against Corruption, Merida, Yucatan, Mexico, December 9–11, 2003, http://www.worldbank.org/wbi/governance/pdf /merida_wbstatement.pdf.

5. World Bank, January 26, 2007, from http://www.worldbank.org/.

6. Simeon Djankov, Rafael La Porta, Florencio Lopez-de-Silanes, and Andrei Schleifer, "Courts: The Lex Mundi Project," National Bureau of Economic Research Working Paper No. 8890, April 2002.

7. Louise I. Shelley, "Organized Crime and Corruption Are Alive and Well in Ukraine," *Beyond Transition: The Newsletter About Reforming Economies* 9/4 August (1998).

8. Djankov, La Porta, Lopez-de-Silanes and Schleifer, "Courts."

9. Jeffrey A. Andrews, "Pfizer's Viagra Patent and the Promise of Patent Protection in China," *Chinese State Intellectual Property Organization v. Pfizer Corp*, 2004, "China's Viagra Heist," *Asian Wall St. Journal,* July 9, 2004.

10. Ibid.

11. Peter Pitts, "Counterfeit Drugs and China," Center for Medicine in the Public Interest, http://www.cmpi.org/newsDetail.asp?contentdetailid=67&content-typeid=3.

12. "Drug Patents Under Attack," *The Economist*, September 7, 2006.

13. Allan Rubin and Harold Rubin, "Patents and Prescription Drugs: Part II," http://www.therubins.com/legal/patext2.htm.

14. "Violation of WTO Trade-Related Aspects of International Property Rights (TRIPS)," specifically Section 7, Article 39.3, U.S. Office of Trade Representative TRIPS 2006 Watch List, 2002. See: http://www.wto.org/english/tratop_e/trips_e/trips_e.htm.

15. The International Intellectual Property Alliance (IIPA) estimates that software piracy in 2005 was 73 percent and losses amounted to $23.6 million. *Economist Intelligence Unit Report, Legal and Regulatory Risk,* Riskwire, April 27, 2007.

16. Ibid.

17. "Constitutional Amendment Benefits the Turkish Power Market," Findlaw Library, Thomson Publishing, Cadwalader, Wiskersham & Taft LLP (1999): 4.

18. For a more complete discussion of the legal failures, see: Ozer Ertuna, "Constraints of Privatization: The Turkish Case," Mediterranean Development Forum, September 3-6, 1998, http://www.worldbank.org/wbi/mdf/mdf2/papers/partnerships/ertuna.pdf; Michael D. Watkins, Banu Ozcan, Burkhard Schrage, and Paul Vaaler, "The Privatization of Anatolia National Telekom," Case 9-801-435, (Boston: Harvard Business School Press, 2001); "Privatization of Turk Telecom," Republic of Turkey Prime Ministry, January 23, 2007.http://www.oib.gov.tr/telekom/turk_telekomunikasyon.htm.

19. Morgan Guaranty Bank, "Privatization Master Plan: Turkey," 1986, Report for State Property Organization.

20. Ertuna, "Constraints of Privatization."

21. "Constitutional Amendment Benefits the Turkish Power Market", Cadwalader, Wiskersham & Taft, LLP, Findlaw Library, 1999.

22. Thailand Petrochemical Industry (TPI), *Annual Report,* 2000.

23. "Infrastructure Development Unlikely to Spur Growth," Indonesia Corruption Watch, February 4, 2005, http://www.antikorupsi.org/eng/mod.php?mod=publisher&op=viewarticle&artid=332.

24. "EU Court Rules France Telecom Broke Antitrust Rules," Reuters, January 30, 2007, http://www.reuters.com/article/technologyNews/idUSBRU00535220070130.

Chapter 5

1. Bloomberg, January 29, 2007.

2. "Auditors in Japan under Attack," *The Economist*, May 11, 2006.

3. K. K. Mwenda and A. Fleming, "International Developments in the Organizational Structure of Financial Services Supervision: Part 1," *Journal of International Banking Law,* Vol. 16, No. 12, 2001; Stephen B. Salter, "Cultural Differences on the Development of Accounting Systems," *Journal of Itnernatioinal Business Studies, 26/1* (1995).

4. For more information, see: http://www.iasb.org; http://www.iosco.org; and http://www.fibv.com.

5. Deborah Orr, "Maxwell's Ghost," *Forbes*, September 9, 2002.

6. "FASB Statements of Financial Accounting Standards (SFAS)," 2006, http://www.fasab.gov/accepted.html .

7. http://www.fasab.gov/accepted.html , 2006.

8. Shivaram Rajgopal, Suresh Kota, Violina Rindova, "Reputation Building and Performance: An Empirical Analysis of the Top 50 Pure Internet Firms," *European Management Journal* 19, no. 6 (2001): 571–586.

9. Bethany McLean (2006). "Judgment Day," *Fortune*, January 11, 2006, 42.

10. Alex Gibney, *Enron: The Smartest Guys in the Room*, HDNet Films, 2005.

11. "Auditors in Japan under Attack."

12. Masao Nakamura, "Japanese corporate governance practices in the post-bubble era: Implications of institutional and legal reforms in the 1990s and early 2000s," *International Journal of Disclosure and Governance, 3/3/* (June 2006):233–261.

13. Helena Tang, Edda Zoli, and Irina Klytchnikova, "Banking Crises in Transition Economies: Fiscal Costs and Related Issues," Policy Research working paper, The World Bank, Washington, DC, 2000.

14. Louis Uchitelle, "The Roulette of Russian Banking," *New York Times*, February 29, 1992.

15. John McMillan and James Twiss, "Gazprom and Hermitage Capital: Shareholder Activism in Russia," Case IB36 (Boston: Harvard Business School Press, 2002).

16. Victor J. Yasmann, "Iran to Get Second Nuclear Reactor from Russia; New Kremlin Spin Doctor Appointed," *Russia Reform Monitor* 827 (March 2001).

17. "Facts About IMF Lending to Russia," International Monetary Fund, September 13, 1999, http://www.imf.org/external/np/vc/1999/091399.HTM.

18. "Ahold Accounting Scandal," Europe.com, September 5, 2003. http://www.foodanddrinkeurope.com/news/ng.asp?id=17477-ahold-accounting-scandal; see also, "Royal Ahold's Royal Holdup," Wharton Research Note, March 23, 2004.

19. *Food and Drink Europe,* September 5, 2003.

20. "Cultural Revolution: Chinese Accounting," *The Economist* (January 11, 2007).

21. Ibid.

Chapter 6

1. *Bloomberg*, January 29, 2007.

2. J. F. Hornbeck, "Argentina's Sovereign Debt Restructuring," CRS Report for Congress, October 19, 2004.

3. Jan Joost Teunissen and Age Akkerman, "The Crisis that Was Not Prevented: Lessons for Argentina, the IMF, and Globalisation," Forum on Debate and Development, February 2003, http://www.fondad.org/catalog/view/10.

4. Roberto Zagha and Gobind T. Nankani, eds., *Economic Growth in the 1990s: Learning from a Decade of Reform* (Washington, DC: World Bank Publications, 2005): 242–251.

5. Crises were often exacerbated by a high loan concentration in closely held family or industrial groups.

6. Thorsten Beck, Ross Levine, and Norman Loayza, "Finance and the Sources of Growth," Policy Research working paper, The Development Research Group, The World Bank, Washington, DC, 1999. http://www.bis.org/publ/bcbs107.htm.

7. Rafael La Porta, Florencio Lopez-de-Silanes, Andrei Schleifer, "Government Ownership of Banks," *The Journal of Finance* 57 (2002): 265–301.

8. For a discussion of the importance of this point, see www.opacity index.com.

9. Basel Committee on Banking Supervision, "Core Principals for Effective Banking Supervision," Bank for International Settlements, October 2006, http://www.bis.org/publ/bcbs129.pdf.

10. "Basel II: International Convergence of Capital Measurement and Capital Standards: A Revised Framework," Bank for International Settlements, June 2004.

11. "Doing Business Survey in 2007: How to Reform," The World Bank, http://www.doingbusiness.org. http://www.doingbusiness.org/Downloads/

12. Stephen L. Kass and Jean M. McCarroll., "The Metalclad Decision Under NAFTA's Chapter 11," *New York Law Journal*, October 27, 2000.

13. Subcommittee on the Western Hemisphere, "United States Trade Disputes in Peru and Ecuador," 2004, http://www.foreignaffairs.house.gov/archives/108/96358.pdf.

14. Ibid.

15. Ibid.

16. "Undermined: Mining in South Africa," *The Economist*, November 16, 2006.

17. Fred McMahon, *Annual Survey of Mining Companies 2004/2005*, The Fraser Institute, http://www.fraserinstitute.ca/admin/books/files/Mining04.pdf.

18. "Chaebol," http://en.wikipedia.org/wiki/Chaebol.

19. "South Korean Conglomerates," *The Economist*, December 11, 1997.

20. Brian Gongol, "South Korean Chaebol (Federation of Korean Industries) Slush Funds in Glovis and Hyundai, Samsung, and LG," 2002, http://www.gongol.com/research/economics/chaebol/.

21. McKinsey & Company, "Global Investor Opinion Survey: Key Findings," July 2002, http://www.mckinsey.com/clientservice/organizationleadership/service/corpgovernance/pdf/GlobalInvestorOpinionSurvey2002.pdf.

Chapter 7

1. "Israel," The World Factbook, https://www.cia.gov/cia/publications/factbook/geos/is.html.

2. Edward Cody, "China growing more wary amid rash of violent protests," *Washington Post*, August 12, 2005.

3. Thomas Lum, "Social Unrest in China," Congressional Research Service, Library of Congress, May 9, 2006.

4. Jane Macartney, "Chinese Censors Tighten Rules to Stop Foreigners Spreading News," *TimesOnline,* September 11, 2006, http://www.timesonline.co.uk/tol/news/world/asia/article635168.ece.

5. "Sri Lanka; Market Offers Prospects for Both Exporters and Investors," *Business America*, September 30, 1985.

6. "Middle East Capital Markets: Market Building, Nation Building," Milken Institute Global Conference 2006, Beverly Hills, CA, 2006.

Chapter 8

1. Department of Enterprise, Trade and Employment, "Tánaiste Announces New Rules to Govern the Accountancy Profession," http://www.entemp.ie/press /2002/130202a.htm.

2. Ian Mackintosh, "The Role of the Accounting Standards Board," Institute of Chartered Accountants Public Meeting, Dublin, Ireland, 2006.

3. "Corruption Perceptions Index 2005," Transparency International, http: //www.transparency.org/policy_research/surveys_indices/cpi/2005.

4. *Wall Street Journal,* September 27, 2006.

5. Annual Report Transparency International, 2005.

6. http://www.boj.or.jp/en/index.htm. Bank of Japan, *Monthly Report of Economic and Financial Developments,* February 1, 2007.

7. Mexican Stock Exchange Commission, Bulletin 11-33, February 2007, http: //www.bmv.com.mx/.

8. "Clifford Krauss, Argentina's Austerity Bill," *New York Times,* July 31, 2001.

9. "Half Year Economic & Fiscal Update 2006," http://www.treasury.govt .nz/forecasts/hyefu/2006/.

10. "New Policy Targets Agreement," Reserve Bank of New Zealand, September 17, 2002, http://www.rbnz.govt.nz/news/2002/0124629.html.

Chapter 9

1. Glenn Yago and James Barth, Tong Li, Sangeetha Malaiyandi, and Triphon Phumiwasana, "Home Bias in Global Capital Markets: What Is the Potential Demand for U.S. Asset-Backed Securities?" Research Report, March 2006, Milken Institute, Santa Monica, CA, 2006.

2. As Jeffrey Williamson writes, "[Prior to World War I] the evolution of well-functioning global markets in goods and labor eventually brought a convergence between nations. This factor price convergence planted, however, seeds for its own destruction since it created rising inequality in labor-scarce economies and falling inequality in labor-abundant economies. The voices of powerful interest groups who were hit hard by these globalization events were heard, however, and these were in particular the ordinary worker in labor scarce economies and the landlord in labor abundant economies. These interest groups generated a political backlash against immigration and trade, and this backlash, which had been building up for decades, was brought to a head by events around World War I." Jeffrey Williamson, "Globalization, Labor Markets and Policy Backlash in the Past," *Journal of Economic Perspectives* 12, no. 4 (Fall 1998).

3. Global Development Finance, International Finance Corporation (2005): 6–7.

4. Glenn Yago, "Private Capital Flows, Emerging Economies, and International Financial Architecture," in *The Bridge to a Global Middle Class: Development, Trade and International Finance*, eds. Walter Russell Mead and Sherle R. Schwenninger (Boston: Kluwer Academic Publishers, 2002).

5. Edmund Phelps, Behind this Structural Boom: The Role of Asset Valuations, *American Economic Review*, 89/2:63–68, 1999.

Selected Bibliography

"About Transparency International: What Is Corruption?" Transparency International, http://transparency.org/about_us.

"Ahold Accounting Scandal," Europe.com, September 5, 2003, http://www.food anddrinkeurope.com/news/ng.asp?id=17477-ahold-accounting-scandal.

Andrews, Jeffrey A., "Pfizer's Viagra Patent and the Promise of Patent Protection in China," *Chinese State Intellectual Property Organization v. Pfizer Corp*, 2004.

Aon Corporation. *Political & Economic Risk Map*, 2006.

Ashby, Tom "Nigerian Oil Security Raised Amid Rebel Threat." Reuters, September 28, 2004.

"Auditors in Japan under Attack," *The Economist*, May 11, 2006.

Bank of Japan, *Monthly Report of Economic and Financial Developments, February 1, 2007*, http://www.boj.or.jp/en/index.htm.

Barrionuevo, Alexei, "The Enron Verdict: The Overview: Two Enron Chiefs Are Convicted in Fraud and Conspiracy Trial," *New York Times*, May 26, 2006.

Barth, James, Tong Li, Sangeetha Malaiyandi, Donald McCarthy, Triphon Phumi-wasana, and Glenn Yago. "Capital Access Index 2005: Best Markets for Entre-preneurial Finance." Research report, Milken Institute, Santa Monica, CA, 2005.

Barth, James R., Dan Brumbaugh, Glenn Yago, and Lalita Rameesh, "The Role of Governments and Markets in International Banking Crises." *Financial Services: Public and Private Policy* 10 (1998): 36-62.

Barth, James. R., Steven Caudill, and Glenn Yago. "Cross-Country Evidence on Banking Crises: Do Financial Structure and Bank Regulation Matter?" In *Bank Fragility and Regulation: Evidence from Different Countries*, edited by G. G. Kauf-man, 3–23. Amsterdam: Elsevier, 2000.

Barth, James R., Tong Li, Don McCarthy, Triphon Phumiwasana, and Glenn Yago, "The Economic Impacts of Global Terrorism: From Munich to Bali," working paper, Milken Institute, Santa Monica, CA, October 2006.

Basel Committee on Banking Supervision, "Core Principals for Effective Banking Supervision," Bank for International Settlements, October 2006, http://www .bis.org/publ/bcbs129.pdf.

"Basel II: International Convergence of Capital Measurement and Capital Standards: A Revised Framework," Bank for International Settlements, June 2004, http://www.bis.org/publ/bcbs107.htm.

Beck, Thorsten, Ross Levine, and Norman Loayza. "Finance and the Sources of Growth." Policy Research working paper, The Development Research Group, The World Bank, Washington, DC, 1999.

Bekaert, Geert, Campbell R. Harvey, and Christian Lundblad. "Liquidity and Expected Returns: Lessons from Emerging Markets." Working paper 11413, National Bureau of Economic Research, Cambridge, MA, 2005.

Bloomberg Terminal, January 29, 2007.

"Bolivia May Clip Wings of LAB," *Prensa Latina*, June 14, 2006.

"China's Viagra Heist," *Asian Wall St. Journal*, July 9, 2004.

"Constitutional Amendment Benefits the Turkish Power Market," Findlaw Library, Thomas Publishing, Cadwalader, Wiskersham & Taft LLP (1999): 4.

"Corruption Perceptions Index 2005," Transparency International, http://www.transparency.org/policy_research/surveys_indices/cpi/2005. "Cultural Revolution: Chinese Accounting." *The Economist*, January 11, 2007.

Department of Enterprise, Trade and Employment, "Tánaiste Announces New Rules to Govern the Accountancy Profession," http://www.entemp.ie/press/2002/130202a.htm.

Djankov, Simeon, Rafael La Porta, Florencio Lopez-de-Silanes, and Andrei Schleifer, "Courts: The Lex Mundi Project," National Bureau of Economic Research Working Paper No. 8890, April 2002.

"Doing Business Survey in 2007: How to Reform," The World Bank, http://www.doingbusiness.org/Downloads/

Dreher, Axel, Christos Kotsogiannis, and Steven McCorriston, "Corruption Around the World: Evidence from a Structural Model." *Public Economics* 5, no. 2 (2004): 305–312.

"Drug Patents Under Attack." *The Economist*, September 9, 2006.

Economist Intelligence Unit Report, Legal and Regulatory Risk, Riskwire, April 27, 2007.

Ertuna, Ozer. "Constraints of Privatization: The Turkish Case." Mediterranean Development Forum, September 3–6, 1998, http://www.worldbank.org/wbi/mdf/mdf2/papers/partnerships/ertuna.pdf.

"EU Court Rules France Telecom Broke Antitrust Rules." Reuters. January 30, 2007. http://www.reuters.com/article/technologyNews/idUSBRU00535220070130.

"Experts Meet to Hone Guide to Financial Soundness Indicators." *IMF Survey* 31, no. 19 (2002): 328–329.

"Facts About IMF Lending to Russia," International Monetary Fund, September 13, 1999, http://www.imf.org/external/np/vc/1999/091399.HTM.

"FASB Statements of Financial Accounting Standards (SFAS)," 2006, http://www.fasab.gov/accepted.html.

Fuentes, Federico, "Evo Morales Confronts New Challenges," ZNet, April 10, 2006, http://www.zmag.org/content/showarticle.cfm?ItemID=10073.

"Germany: Auditors Detail VW Corruption in India and Czech Republic." Corp-Watch. November 11, 2005. http://www.corpwatch.org/article.php?id=12772.

Gibney, Alex, *Enron: The Smartest Guys in the Room*, HDNet Films, 2005.

Glahe, Fred R., (ed.), *Keynes's The General Theory of Employment, Interest, and Money: A Concordance*. Savage, MD: Rowman & Littlefield, 1991.

Global Development Finance. International Finance Corporation (2005): 6–7.

Gong, Ting. "Forms and Characteristics of China's Corruption in the 1990s: Change with Continuity." *Communist and Post-Communist Studies* 30 (1997): 277–288.

Gongol, Brian, "South Korean Chaebol (Federation of Korean Industries) Slush Funds in Glovis and Hyundai, Samsung, and LG," 2002.

Gould, Jens Erik. "Venezuela Disavows 1980s-Era Bonds." *New York Times*, March 7, 2007.

"Half Year Economic & Fiscal Update 2006," http://www.treasury.govt.nz/forecasts /hyefu/2006/.

Home Office, Foreign and Commonwealth Minister, Report on Drug Trafficking in Kenya and its Effect on Britain." Foreign and Commonwealth Office, 2006.

Honohan, Patrick, and Daniela Klingebiel. "Controlling the Fiscal Costs of Banking Crises." In "Managing the Real and Fiscal Effects of Banking Crises," edited by Daniela Klingebiel and Luc Laeven. Discussion paper 428, World Bank, Washington, DC, 2002.

Hornbeck, J. F., "Argentina's Sovereign Debt Restructuring," CRS Report for Congress, October 19, 2004.

Hope, Kerin, and Theodor Troev. "Bulgaria: Corruption Is Still a Key Stumbling Block." *Financial Times Limited,* May 19, 2006.

"Infrastructure Development Unlikely to Spur Growth," Indonesia Corruption Watch, February 4, 2005, http://www.antikorupsi.org/eng/mod.php?mod =publisher&op=viewarticle&artid=332.

International Monetary Fund. 2005 World Economic Outlook Database. Washington, DC: International Monetary Fund, 2005.

International Monetary Fund. "Facts About IMF Lending to Russia." September 13, 1999, http://www.imf.org/external/np/vc/1999/091399.HTM.

International Monetary Fund. *International Financial Statistics.* Washington, DC: International Monetary Fund, 2001.

"Israel," The World Factbook, https://www.cia.gov/cia/publications/factbook/geos /is.html.

Johnson, David T. "Bureaucratic Corruption in Japan." Working paper 76, Japan Policy Research Institute, Encinitas, CA, 2001.

Johnson, David T. *The Japanese Way of Justice: Prosecuting Crime in Japan (Studies on Law and Social Control).* New York: Oxford University Press, 2005.

Kass, Stephen L., and Jean M. McCarroll., "The Metalclad Decision Under NAFTA's Chapter 11," *New York Law Journal*, October 27, 2000.

Kaufmann, Daniel. "Anti-Corruption within a Broader Developmental and Governance Perspective: Some Lessons from Empirics and Experience." Statement by Head of the World Bank Delegation to the High Level Political Signing Conference for the United Nations Convention Against Corruption, Merida, Yucatan, Mexico, December 9–11, 2003, http://www.worldbank.org/wbi/governance/pdf /merida_wbstatement.pdf.

Kaufmann, Daniel. "Myths and Realities of Governance and Corruption," World Bank, Washington, DC, 2003.

Krauss, Clifford, Argentina's Austerity Bill," *New York Times*, July 31, 2001.

Kurtzman, Joel, Glenn Yago, and Triphon Phumiwasana. "The Global Costs of Opacity." *MIT Sloan Management Review* 46, no. 1 (2004): 38–44.

Leeson, Peter T. and Russell S. Sobel. "The Impact of FEMA on U.S. Corruption: Implications for Policy." Mercatus Center, George Mason University, January 11, 2007, http://www.mercatus.org/repository/docLib/20070111_The_Impact _of_FEMA_on_US_Corruption.pdf

Lum, Thomas,"Social Unrest in China," Congressional Research Service, Library of Congress, May 9, 2006.

Macartney, Jane, "Chinese Censors Tighten Rules to Stop Foreigners Spreading News," TimesOnline, September 11, 2006, http://www.timesonline.co.uk/tol /news/world/asia/article635168.ece.

Mackintosh, Ian, "The Role of the Accounting Standards Board," Institute of Chartered Accountants Public Meeting, Dublin, Ireland, 2006.

McCoy, Jennifer L. and David J. Myers, eds. *The Unraveling of Representative Democracy in Venezuela*. Baltimore, MD: Johns Hopkins University Press, 2004.

McGovern, Kat, 2003. *Ethnicity, conflict and peacebuilding: the case of the Solomon Islands*. Unpublished MA Thesis, International Relations and Asian Politics Department, University of Queensland.

McKinsey & Company. "Global Investor Opinion Survey: Key Findings." July 2002, http://www.mckinsey.com/clientservice/organizationleadership/service/corp governance/pdf/GlobalInvestorOpinionSurvey2002.pdf.

McLean, Bethany. "Judgment Day," Fortune, January 11, 2006, 42.

McMahon, Fred. *Annual Survey of Mining Companies 2004/2005*, The Fraser Institute, http://www.fraserinstitute.ca/admin/books/files/Mining04.pdf.

McMillan, John, and James Twiss, "Gazprom and Hermitage Capital: Shareholder Activism in Russia," Case IB36 (Boston: Harvard Business School, 2002).

Mexican Stock Exchange Commission, Bulletin 11-33, February 2007, http://www .bmv.com.mx/.

"Middle East Capital Markets: Market Building, Nation Building," Milken Institute Global Conference 2006, Beverly Hills, CA, 2006.

Monnet, Cyrill, and Warren E. Weber, "Money and Interest Rates," *Federal Reserve Bank of Minneapolis Quarterly Review* 25/4 (Fall 2001).

Morales, Evo. "We Need Partners, Not Bosses." Address to the United Nations, September 22, 2006.

Morgan Guaranty Bank, "Privatization Master Plan: Turkey," Report for State Property Organization, 1986.

Mwenda, K.K., and A. Fleming, "International Developments in the Organizational Structure of Financial Services Supervision: Part 1," Journal of International Banking Law, Vol. 16, No. 12, 2001; Stephen B. Salter, "Cultural Differences on the Development of Accounting Systems," *Journal of Itnernatioinal Business Studies, 26/1* (1995).

Nakamura, Masao, "Japanese corporate governance practices in the post-bubble era: Implications of institutional and legal reforms in the 1990s and early 2000s," *International Journal of Disclosure and Governance, 3/3* (June 2006): 233–261.

Nally, Dennis. "PricewaterhouseCoopers' CEO Survey." PricewaterhouseCoopers, LLC, 2005.

"New Policy Targets Agreement," Reserve Bank of New Zealand, September 17, 2002, http://www.rbnz.govt.nz/news/2002/0124629.html.

O'Donnell, Jayne, and Andrew Backover. "Ebbers' High-Risk Act Came Crashing Down on Him." *USA Today*, December 11, 2002.

Organization for Economic Co-operation and Development. "United Kingdom: Phase 2 Report on the Application of the Convention on Combating Bribery of Public Officials in International Business Transactions and the 1997 Recommendation on Combating Bribery in International Business Transactions." April 12, 2007, http://www.oecd.org/dataoecd/62/32/34599062.pdf.

Orr, Deborah, "Maxwell's Ghost," *Forbes*, September 9, 2002.

Phelps, Edmund. Behind this Structural Boom: The Role of Asset Valuations. *American Economic Review,* 89/2: 63-68,1999.

Pitts, Peter. "Counterfeit Drugs and China." Center for Medicine in the Public Interest, http://www.cmpi.org/newsDetail.asp?contentdetailid=67&contenttypeid=3.

Polgreen, Lydia. "Nigeria: High-Level Bribery Scandal." *New York Times*, March 23, 2005.

Porter, Michael E., Klaus Schwab, Xavier Sala-I-Martin, and Augusto Lopez-Claros, eds. *The Global Competitiveness Report 2003–2004.* New York: Palgrave Macmillan, 2005.

"Privatization Master Plan: Turkey." Morgan Guaranty Bank, 1986.

"Privatization of Turk Telecom." Republic of Turkey Prime Ministry, http://www.oib.gov.tr/telekom/turk_telekomunikasyon.htm.

Rajgopal, Shivaram, Suresh Kota, Violina Rindova, "Reputation Building and Performance: An Empirical Analysis of the Top 50 Pure Internet Firms," *European Management Journal* 19, no. 6 (2001): 571–586.

Rohter, Larry. "A Leftist Surges in Brazil's Turbulent Presidential Election." *New York Times*, May 17, 2002.

Roque, Josephine. January 16, 2007, "Former VW Boss Faces Corruption Case," http://www.allheadlinenews.com/articles/7006158409.

Roubini, Nouriel, and Xavier Sala-I-Martin, "A Growth Model of Inflation, Tax Evasion, and Financial Repression," working paper W4062, National Bureau of Economic Research, Cambridge, MA, 1992.

"Royal Ahold's Royal Holdup," Wharton Research Note, March 23, 2004.

Rubin, Allan, and Harold Rubin. "Patents and Prescription Drugs: Part II," http://www .therubins.com/legal/patext2.htm.

Shelley, Louise I., "Organized Crime and Corruption Are Alive and Well in Ukraine," *Beyond Transition: The Newsletter About Reforming Economies*, 9/4 August (1998).

"South Korean Conglomerates," *The Economist*, December 11, 1997.

"Sri Lanka; Market Offers Prospects for Both Exporters and Investors," *Business America*, September 30, 1985.

Subcommittee on the Western Hemisphere, "United States Trade Disputes in Peru and Ecuador (Washington, DC: GPO, 2004), http://www.foreignaffairs.house .gov/archives/108/96358.pdf.

Tang, Helena, Edda Zoli, and Irina Klytchnikova, "Banking Crises in Transition Economies: Fiscal Costs and Related Issues," Policy Research working paper, The World Bank, Washington, DC, 2000.

Teunissen, Jan Joost and Age Akkerman, "The Crisis that Was Not Prevented: Lessons for Argentina, the IMF, and Globalisation," Forum on Debate and Development, February 2003, http://www.fondad.org/catalog/view/10.

Thailand Petrochemical Industry (TPI), *Annual Report,* 2000.

Transparency International. "Corruption Perceptions Index 2005," http://www .transparency.org/policy_research/surveys_indices/cpi/2005.

Uchitelle, Louis, "The Roulette of Russian Banking," *New York Times*, February 29, 1992.

"U.N. Report Reinforces Security Council Divisions," CNN.com, February 14, 2003, http://www.cnn.com/2003/US/02/14/sprj.irq.un/index.html.

Uhlenbruck, Klaus, Peter Rodriguez, Jonathan Doh, and Lorraine Eden, *Global Corruption Report 2005*. Berlin: Transparency International, 2005.

"Undermined: Mining in South Africa." *The Economist*, November 16, 2006.

U.S. Congress. *Sarbanes-Oxley Act of 2002*. HR 3763. 107th Congress. July 30, 2002.

U.S. Department of Justice. *Foreign Corrupt Practices Act of 1977*. 2000. 15 U.S.C.

"Violation of WTO Trade-Related Aspects of International Property Rights (TRIPS)," specifically Section 7, Article 39.3, U.S. Office of Trade Representative TRIPS 2006 Watch List, 2002, http://www.wto.org/english/tratop_e/trips_ e/trips_e.htm.

Volcker, Paul. "The Management of the United Nations Oil-for-Food Programme: Volume III, Report of Investigation," September 7, 2005, http://www.iic-offp.org /documents/Sept05/Mgmt_V3.pdf.

Wagner, Wolf. Diversification at Financial Institutions and Systemic Crises, Discussion Paper 72. Tilburg University, Center for Economic Research, 2006.

Watkins, Michael D., Banu Ozcan, Burkhard Schrage, and Paul Vaaler. "The Privatization of Anatolia National Telekom." Case 9-801-435. Boston: Harvard Business School Press, 2001.

Wei, Shang-Jin. "How Taxing Is Corruption on International Investors?" *Review of Economics and Statistics* 82, no. 1 (2000): 11.

Wei, Shang-Jin. "Domestic Crony Capitalism and International Fickle Capital: Is There a Connection?" *International Finance* 4, no. 1 (2001): 15–45.

Williamson, Jeffrey. "Globalization, Labor Markets and Policy Backlash in the Past." *Journal of Economic Perspectives* 12, no. 4 (Fall 1998).

Wood, D. "Convening Report: Toward a Coherent Investment Framework for Sustainability Investing in Small and Medium Sized Enterprises in the Developing World." *Sustainability Investing in Small and Medium Sized Enterprises in the Developing World.* Boston: Boston College, 2006.

Yago, Glenn. "Private Capital Flows, Emerging Economies, and International Financial Architecture." In *The Bridge to a Global Middle Class: Development, Trade and International Finance*, edited by Walter Russell Mead and Sherle R. Schwenninger, 85-124. Boston: Kluwer Academic Publishers, 2002.

Yago, Glenn, James Barth, Tong Li, Sangeetha Malaiyandi, and Triphon Phumiwasana. "Home Bias in Global Capital Markets: What Is the Potential Demand for U.S. Asset-Backed Securities?" Research Report, March 2006, Milken Institute, Santa Monica, CA, 2006.

Yasmann, Victor J., "Iran to Get Second Nuclear Reactor from Russia; New Kremlin Spin Doctor Appointed," *Russia Reform Monitor* 827 (March 2001).

Zagha, Roberto and Gobind T. Nankani, eds., *Economic Growth in the 1990s: Learning from a Decade of Reform* (Washington, DC: World Bank Publications, 2005): 242–251.

Index

About the Authors

Joel Kurtzman is a senior fellow at the Milken Institute and a principle at The Kurtzman Group, an international advisory firm. He is also a senior advisor to Knowledge Universe. Kurtzman is former global lead partner for thought leadership and innovation at PricewaterhouseCoopers, and an alliance partner with Booz Allen Hamilton. He has served as a consultant to some of the world's largest companies in various business sectors. Kurtzman is the former Editor of the *Harvard Business Review* and former business editor and columnist at the *New York Times*. Earlier in his career, Joel was an international economist at the United Nations, where he was deputy director of the UN's Project on the Future. His economic modeling teams were the first to warn of the impending Latin America debt crisis. While at the UN, Joel was a negotiator between India and the Union Carbide Corporation over the Bhopal disaster. He was awarded India's Indira Gandhi Prize for these efforts. Kurtzman is a member of the editorial board of MIT's *Sloan Management Review*. He speaks to diverse business and government audiences around the world, has hosted television and radio programs globally, and has served as chairman of numerous conferences. He is the author of twenty books and hundreds of articles. http://www.kurtzmangroup.com

Glenn Yago is Director of Capital Studies at the Milken Institute and a leading authority on financial innovations, capital markets, emerging markets, and environmental finance. He is also a senior

Koret Knesset fellow, directing postgraduate research on economic and financial reform at the Jerusalem Center for Public Affairs in Israel. Yago focuses on the innovative use of financial instruments to solve long-standing economic development, social, and environmental challenges. His work has contributed to policy innovations fostering the democratization of capital to traditionally underserved markets and entrepreneurs in the United States and around the world. Prior to joining the Milken Institute, Yago served as a professor at the State University of New York at Stony Brook and at the City University of New York Graduate Center PhD Program in Economics. He has also taught at Tel Aviv University and the Interdisciplinary Center-Herzliya. In 2002, Yago received the Gleitsman Foundation Award of Achievement for social change. He has a PhD from the University of Wisconsin, Madison. http://www.milkeninstitute.org